INNOVATIVE HOUSES
Concepts for Sustainable Living

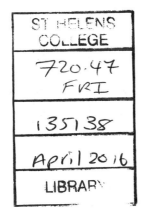

LAURENCE KING

Published in 2013
by Laurence King Publishing Ltd
361–373 City Road
London EC1V 1LR
Tel +44 20 7841 6900
Fax +44 20 7841 6910
E enquiries@laurenceking.com
www.laurenceking.com

Reprinted 2014

ISBN 978 1 78067 293 9

Designed by The Urban Ant Ltd
Research assistants: Jack Bian and Dave Cameron
Coordinator: Nyd Garavito-Bruhn
Project editor: Gaynor Sermon
Printed in China

INNOVATIVE HOUSES
Concepts for Sustainable Living

Avi Friedman

Laurence King Publishing

CONTENTS

ACKNOWLEDGMENTS

The seed of the idea for the writing of this book was planted in an Innovative Housing seminar that I taught at McGill University; many thanks to the students who inspired my ideas. Those ideas were also the outcome of work with colleagues and graduate students with whom I authored papers and designed prototypes. I thank them all.

The book could not have been written without the help of a highly dedicated team of assistants: Ji (Cayte) Yeon Kim helped put together the proposal. Jack Bian and Dave Cameron contributed to the background research, the writing of the text, finding the projects and describing them. Their work was made possible through the Summer Undergraduate Research in Engineering (SURE) programme of the Faculty of Engineering at McGill University.

Special thanks go to Nyd Garavito-Bruhn, my assistant, who assembled and formatted the text and the images, coordinated the assembly of the projects, and processed the graphic material. His dedication is much appreciated.

Gratitude is also given to the team at Laurence King Publishing for their care and, in particular, to Editorial Director Philip Cooper, for ushering in the project, and to Project Editor Gaynor Sermon for guiding it through the different production stages.

Finally, to my wife Sorel Friedman and children Paloma, who edited the text, and Ben, for their love and support.

PREFACE

The beginning of the twenty-first century launched a 'perfect storm' of societal changes that are bound to affect the way that people around the world will house themselves in the coming decades. Among the principal attributes leading these changes is the transformation of the family and the rise of the non-traditional household, whose composition is markedly different and smaller than it was just half a century ago. The current era is also marked by a rise in the numbers of elderly people in most nations. Parallel to these demographic changes, new lifestyle habits have led to an interest in new housing prototypes whose interior arrangement no longer resembles older dwellings.

The rise in construction costs has put owning dwellings beyond the reach of many. It has made it especially hard for first-time buyers to become homeowners in most of the world's urban centres. The need to develop new and efficient design and production methods, and to replace outdated paradigms is therefore paramount. Designers and builders are now exploring expandable and adaptable units that include, for example, cost-reduction strategies.

Global and local environmental concerns have also propelled themselves to the top of the societal priority list. Climate change, depletion of natural resources and the rise in the cost of energy has affected many nations and individuals. Designing residential environments that address those issues is rapidly becoming a priority. Homes that do not rely on external sources of power, or that use the sun as their main power source, are increasingly being considered. Attention is also being paid to the relationship between dwellings and their surroundings; building with nature in mind, conserving natural habitats and incorporating private gardens in which to grow food are some of the practices being adopted.

This book discusses and illustrates recent, notable residential design trends. The book is organized into four broad areas of interest that in turn are divided into 20 chapters. Each chapter includes an essay, which lays out principles, methods and practices of the subject being discussed. It also includes contemporary projects that illustrate the approach that various architects have followed while designing unique residences. Using text, illustrations and photography, provided by a number of architectural practices, the book is not limited to ideas, but also demonstrates how they can be applied. It offers a comprehensive collection of strategies and examples that are intended to inspire a much-needed innovation in housing design.

Recent changes to the demographic composition of society have affected the ways people live and house themselves. The post-World War II image of the family, made up of a breadwinner father, stay-at-home mother and dependent children, was so persuasive that home builders could easily – and successfully – view the bulk of their potential clientele as a homogeneous buying block. A rapidly changing societal make-up and the emergence of new lifestyle trends have created demands for contemporary housing types that are small, flexible and efficient. Paramount among those changes is the rise of non-traditional and small households. The number of single, childless couples and single-headed families has increased several-fold in the past half century, meriting reconsideration of common housing prototypes.

In addition, the average age of the population in most nations has constantly been on the rise. The numbers of those aged 65 and over have more than doubled since the 1970s. This has created a market demand for accessible and adaptable dwelling forms and other living arrangements in response to senior citizens' needs. The population involved in these changes has reached a critical mass, which validates the alternative approaches being explored by policy makers, designers and developers. Four dwelling concepts that respond to these social transformations are outlined in this section.

Chapter 1
LIVE-WORK RESIDENCES

The digital revolution of the 1980s led to a significant increase in the number of home-based businesses. In 2007, 24.4 million Americans worked either full-time or part-time from home, double the numbers recorded in 1990 (Penn 2007, Lee and Mather 2008). Furthermore, the US-based International Data Corporation estimates that nearly 2 million home-based businesses will be added by 2015 (Jaffe 2011). As result of economic shift, the future, some argue, could see the dispersal of work from traditional offices to homes.

The surge of live–work situations, which is also called 'telecommuting', can be attributed to the advantages that one gets from setting up such an office. Working from home offers a sense of freedom and flexible time management to the worker. It also eliminates the cost, stress and loss of time associated with commuting, leaving more time to pursue leisure activities. The question is: how can a live–work residence be designed to enhance both productivity and family life?

Integrating office and home can be a delicate task, since combining them can lead to a sense of entrapment, distractions and decreased productivity. When properly designed though, a home office can achieve the opposite, and seamlessly integrate work and family life. Factors such as noise, light, air quality and privacy must all be correctly balanced. The challenge of designing a successful live–work environment however, lies in the fact that a desirable home office has to do with programmatic requirements. An office designed for one telecommuter might be a single room, while other home offices might need to accommodate several employees and require both work areas and meeting rooms. In addition, some home businesses can operate retail outlets and so need visual and sound separation between the living and work spaces. Size is another programmatic issue. The type of work may dictate whether the office is an auxiliary structure, an entire floor or just a corner of a room.

One of the primary tools that designers use to create successful workspaces is separation. Most agree that work requires a space of its own, separate from other household activities (Senbel 1995, Dietsch 2008). Some designers have addressed this by creating a work area set apart from the primary living spaces by using passageways or staircases. If a larger office for multiple employees is needed, it is common to

Figure 1.1: Possible locations of a home office in a dwelling.

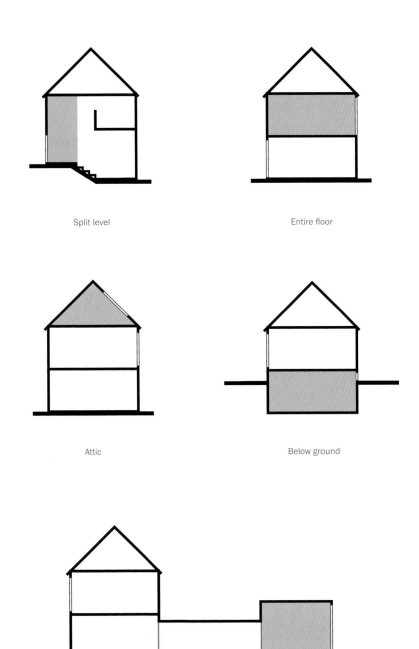

Split level

Entire floor

Attic

Below ground

Ancillary structure

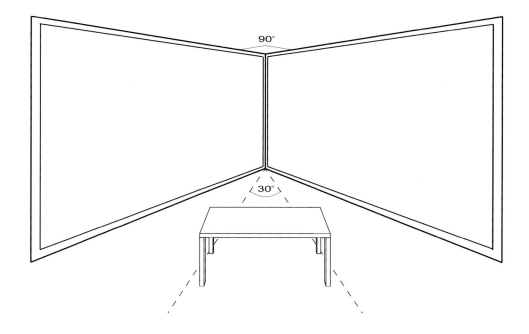

designate an entire level to be the office, typically the ground floor. If the homeowner wants to have a closer connection between the office and family spaces, then a split-level design can be suggested. This vertical division creates a visual separation, yet permits communication among household members in the different sections. At times, noise can become a distraction and therefore the split-level solution is only recommended in quieter situations. For smaller houses, interior dividers or partition walls that form workstations can also be used. The advantage of this approach is that these dividers can be moved around to reconfigure the work areas.

Beyond separating workspaces, there are other methods to improve working conditions in an office. In those with multiple workers, circulation is crucial to the cross fertilization of ideas. Recent studies have shown that an open-plan design allows for spontaneous discussions and for ideas to emerge (Becker and Steele 1995). Separating workspaces from one another in an attempt to increase efficiency may lead to the disruption of communication. Establishing distinct activity zones within the office is also a tool used by designers to create environments that encourage workers to move around. An office can be designed to feel open – which can be achieved by having two-storey spaces – and this can result in many arrangements, such as placing the office in a loft, or below the primary living spaces.

Placing offices near the facade with the most sun exposure is also important. According to studies, letting in ample natural light enhances productivity and feelings of well-being. Windows

Figure 1.2 The work space of a home office should be located in a glare-free area.

in those rooms should, however, be equipped with blinds to reduce extreme brightness and glare, and surface materials should preferably be non-reflective.

Where to locate the entrance to an office is another important decision a designer has to make. In some cases, the office may have its own independent entrance to allow maximum separation. This is usually done when the office has multiple employees or if it is a retail outlet. In other cases, the office can share an entrance with the residence. Although there is a lot of versatility in the design of entrances, most designers argue that there should only be a single entrance into a workspace for better internal circulation.

Due to ongoing economic shifts and further development in digital communication working at home is likely to become more common. All of this means that the design of live–work environments is a rapidly evolving area

DRIVING FORCES

- Economic shifts
- Avoid commute
- Advances in digital communication
- Flexible time management

INNOVATIONS

- Flexibility to accommodate one or several employees
- Flexibility to locate in various spots in the dwelling
- Use of demountable partitions
- Creating a separate entrance to the office

1.1 LIVE-WORK RESIDENCES

Project	House S
Location	Breda, The Netherlands
Architect	Grosfeld van der Velde Architects

House S, with a floor area of 288 m² (3,100 sq ft) over two levels, is built on a sandy hill overlooking the sea in the city of Breda in the Netherlands. The box-like house offers a scenic exterior view from the upper-level living spaces. The home office is located in the basement, where the owner works and meets clients.

The Dutch firm Grosfeld van der Velde Achitecten, who designed the building, placed the living area above ground to enhance both the relationship with nature and productivity. The intention behind the design was to distinctly separate the living and work areas so that each remains undisturbed by the other.

The below-ground working area contains an office space and a

Below: Sections showing the location of the basement office.

Bottom: The profile of the house was lowered by setting in-ground.

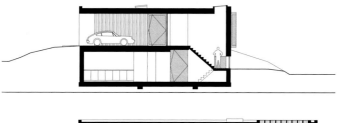

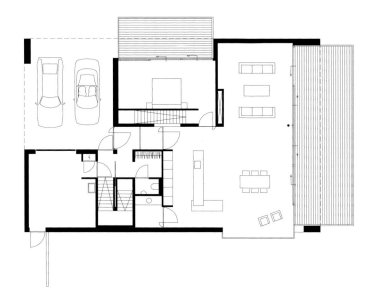

Left: Ground floor – A glass wall offers a panoramic view and lets light into the living room.

Below: Basement – The home office has a direct entrance from above.

Bottom: Site plan.

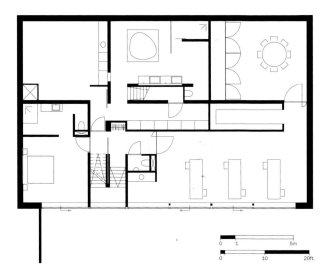

| 0 | 1 | | 5m |
| 0 | | 10 | 20ft. |

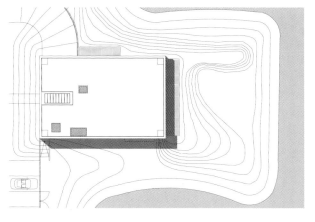

Top left: Side view showing integration of the site and the dwelling.

Bottom Left: View of patio.

meeting room. A long horizontal window provides a scenic view and lets in natural light during daytime. Employees and visitors use a direct entrance to the office, where workstations accommodate them. The meeting room is connected to the office, but it has a more intimate setting and a wall-to-wall storage area.

The house does not have one main staircase; instead, multiple stairways offer separate connections between the two floors to enhance privacy. A glass door divides the private areas from the work rooms, marking them out as distinct, separate spaces without emphasizing the visual connection and continuity of light from one space to another. These design features allow the visual integration of the private and the public realms without them actually crossing each other.

At the end of a work day, the occupants can ascend into the living spaces where the large floor-to-ceiling windows offer a panoramic view of the surroundings. With natural light and an adjacent open terrace, the architect has created a relaxed environment by exposing the occupants to views of the landscape, water and sky.

Top: The house's front elevation.

Above: The panoramic view from the dining area.

1.2 LIVE-WORK RESIDENCES

Project	Intexure Live-Work Studio
Location	Houston, Texas, USA
Architect	Intexure Architects

Russell and Rame Hruska designed the building that houses both their architectural company and their family home. Situated on a vacant infill lot in Houston, Texas, the new building saw their firm, Intexure, move from a downtown warehouse to an urban neighbourhood. The design combines a studio on the ground floor with living space on the first floor. With the ability to substitute travel time for telecommuting and incorporate 'green' construction principles, they show genuine commitment to sustainable living in an automobile-dependent city like Houston.

The two-storey home, which measures 204 m² (2,200 sq ft), is minimally decorated and uses locally purchased materials such as steel columns and wooden floor and ceiling coverings. The

Below: South-east facade showing the living space below and the office above.

Top: Site plan showing the main entrance.

Middle: The two-storey tall work area.

Bottom: The ground floor living area where the dining room can also serve for meetings.

south-orientated studio takes advantage of natural light while also using passive solar design strategies to gain heat in the winter and avoid the summer sun. The office's two-storey tall ceiling and wall-to-wall windows create an open space and also provide a work area for up to 12 employees. Spaces such as the second floor materials library were created as multipurpose areas: during the day, the table could accommodate a meeting overlooking the office space below, while in the evening, it could be used as a dining table for the family. The second floor kitchen offers flexibility because one can prepare a meal without interrupting activities in the working spaces.

The architects incorporated several green technologies in the design. For example, the LEED-certified house includes photovoltaic panels and a rainwater-collection system. In addition, the facade is clad with recycled materials that were sourced within 805 km (500 miles) whenever possible.

Below left: The large window area lets daylight into the work area.

Below right: The well-positioned stairs that connect the living and work areas.

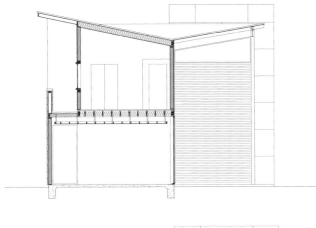

Top and centre: Two principal sections, showing the angled roof, which was designed for water collection.

Bottom: Side view showing the well-illuminated living area.

Chapter 2
AGEING IN PLACE

Declining birthrates, longer life expectancy and the ageing of the 'baby boom' generation have increased the number of senior citizens – those 65 years and over – in most Western societies. In countries such as Japan and Italy, their numbers are projected to account for up to 40 per cent of the population (CSIS 2011). This large-scale increase is expected to put strain on younger taxpayers in order to sustain social services. In 1950, there were 12 working people for every senior citizen in the world. By 2010, that ratio had dropped to 9 to 1 and is expected to drop further, to 4 to 1, by 2050 (PRB 2008). Contributions to health care and social security programmes are also expected to rise as a result of this demographic shift. In the USA, for example, the share of the Gross Domestic Product (GDP) used to finance Medicare and Social Security has risen by 4 per cent since 1970, and is expected to rise further, to 15 per cent, by 2050 (PRB 2008).

Contrary to popular belief, few senior citizens live or wish to live in assisted living arrangements. According to polls, the majority of middle-aged and elderly people plan to spend the rest of their lives in their own home rather than move to an institutional care facility (Lawlor and Thomas 2008). Many private residences, however, are not designed to respond to the needs of an ageing person. Physical conditions caused by ageing and mental health deterioration can, at times, lead to accidents.

'Ageing in place' is a design concept that seeks to create barrier-free spaces that simplify daily tasks for those with reduced mobility and poor vision. Furthermore, senior citizen-friendly homes allow occupants to live on their own for longer, thereby reducing the need for costly support from families and the government (Salomon 2010).

Along with addressing the health of the economy, according to Lawlor and Thomas (2008), ageing in place also addresses one of the four fundamental psychological needs of people: independence. Typically, senior citizens – especially those who were previously very active – have problems adjusting to the physical limitations of an ageing body and still strive to lead a dynamic and socially active life. Studies have shown that successful designs for ageing in place, which allow senior citizens to remain autonomous, can improve their self-esteem, sense of purpose, community contribution and health (Salomon 2010). Since independent living leads to both a positive mental attitude and improved health, ageing in place designs not only benefit the occupants, but also society at large.

The ageing process is long and complex and because predicting all of the conditions that a senior citizen might encounter is difficult, there are many considerations that a designer must address early on. Conditions such as crippling arthritis, loss of vision, leg strength, stability and hearing – to name just a few – present uniquely different challenges to a designer. Furthermore, the house must initially be prepared for the aged when they are designed but before the preparations are actually needed by the occupants. A young couple will not want grab bars in their bathroom, but could wisely plan the means for their installation at a later stage. Another example is to design wider doorframes to accommodate the future use of walkers and wheelchairs, which is less costly if done early on. Housing needs to evolve and adapt easily and cheaply as the occupants' requirements change.

One of the key issues that a designer needs to consider is fall

Figure 2.1 Assistive devices for people with reduced mobility.

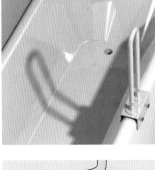

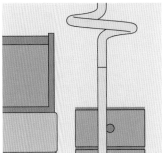
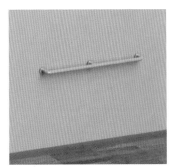

prevention. In the US alone, falls are the second leading cause of injury-related deaths among senior citizens aged 55 to 79 (Lawlor and Thomas 2008). Obstacles, stairs, poor lighting and circulation and level changes in the building may cause such falls. Indoors, objects that can become obstacles should be kept to a minimum and placed along the walls, leaving central spaces free for circulation. In the bedroom, for example, a clear, obstacle-free path from the bed to the bathroom needs to be provided. It is also recommended that every room, including kitchens and bathrooms, have a minimum of a 1.5 m (5 ft) diameter circle of open space in the centre to compensate for reduced peripheral vision and potential wheelchair access.

Joins between internal and external flooring levels and materials should be made smooth and even to prevent trips and falls. Furthermore, different elevations from room to room should be avoided, since they become hazardous as the occupant's vision deteriorates. Having circulation space without sharp corners or turns is also recommended because it facilitates visual and oral communication should an occupant ever require urgent assistance. Good circulation design also allows for spaces that are wider than 81 cm (32 in) to permit wheelchair access. This access width is highly recommended – and at times mandatory – in every ageing in place design because it is of benefit to the occupants as they age, as well as to any visitors who might also require mobility assistance. Rooms, such as bathrooms and kitchens, with tiled floors and any rooms with wooden floor coverings should initially be designed with non-slip floors using wall-to-wall carpets or grooved flooring.

When stairs are included in a design, they need to be carefully planned. Primary living spaces should all be placed on the entrance level to minimize the use of stairs. If having a master bedroom on the ground level is not initially desired, the house should be designed to allow for such a transformation later on. Also, the stairs should have a solid handrail and be wide enough to accommodate a stairlift should one be needed later. The lower and top landings of the staircase should also be open, clear and visible to avoid accidents.

Some rooms may require more attention than others. The most important being the bathroom, bedroom and kitchen, which all require specialized appliances and aids. Facilities such as grab bars, extended bath ledges, walk-in showers, elevated dishwashers, adjustable cabinets and counters and knee spaces under sinks can greatly reduce back stress and slips. There are many innovative fixtures and appliances that can enable ageing in place and when planning such a home, designers should carefully consider them.

Windows and balconies can also be used by designers to enhance the quality of life for occupants of ageing in place designs. Large, well-placed windows can reduce feelings of isolation by permitting a street view of people and nature, while

DRIVING FORCES

- Dramatic increase in the number of seniors
- Longer life expectancy
- Most seniors wish to age in their homes
- Technological developments

INNOVATIONS

- Design to accommodate several ageing stages
- Building initially for later adaptation
- Remote control technologies and robotics
- Flexible kitchen cabinets and storage

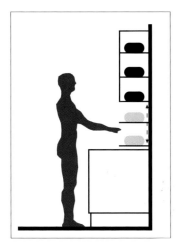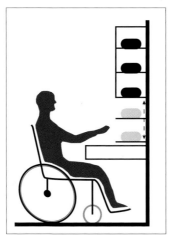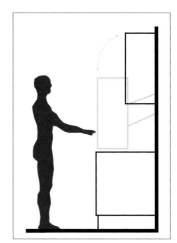

balconies allow occupants to get out in the fresh air and be in touch with others. It is also important to incorporate direct contact with nature indoors, since studies show that visual and physical proximity to the natural world improves mental health (Louv 2005). This can be done through the addition of sunrooms, plants and vegetation or water.

Although there are already many contemporary ageing in place applications, the future seems to lie in smart technologies. Such house designs use digital and electronic systems to aid residents in performing daily tasks, which is especially helpful for senior citizens with reduced motor capabilities. Assistive technologies such as light clappers, remote control operated blinds and automatic doors already exist while others are still in the development phase (ICOST 2010). Furthermore, as the personal robot market is predicted to reach sales of US$19 billion in 2017, one can expect robots to be more common in the future (ABI Research 2010).

Figure 2.2 Adjustable kitchen cabinets for easy reach.

2.1 AGEING IN PLACE

Project	Villa Deys
Location	Rhenen, The Netherlands
Architect	Architectural Office Paul de Ruiter BV

Nestled in an attractive setting in the Netherlands, Villa Deys, designed by architect Paul de Ruiter, blends in nicely with its environment. Conceived as a design for a couple in their sixties, who wish to continue to reside in the same house at an older age, the one-storey, 344 m² (3,703 sq ft) home with its simple design and clever use of materials is barely perceptible within the landscape. The structure merges into the grassland and its gabioned facade resembles the design of traditional Dutch farmhouses.

The interior responds to the functional needs of the occupants. With a love for fitness and swimming, the integration of an indoor pool was one of the client's primary wishes for the house. The centrally located pool is safe for both the occupants and their visiting grandchildren and is protected by glass panels that can be locked up. Along with the vast amounts of light that enter from both ends of the house, the water and its reflections can be seen in the living areas, contributing to the relaxing atmosphere.

The living spaces are located around the pool and the open-plan design allows them to flow nicely into one another. The living room, kitchen and study are orientated to the south, with adjustable blinds to control the intensity of the penetrating light.

Above: The wooden blinds in the southern facade can form a porch above the terrace.

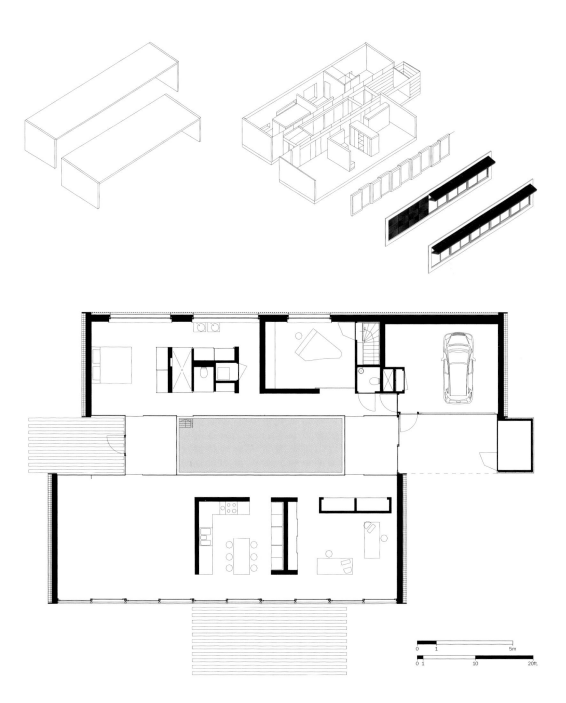

Top left: The two roof plates that make up the dwelling's two sections.

Top right: The home can be regarded as two elongated boxes separated by a swimming pool.

Above: The living spaces are located around the pool.

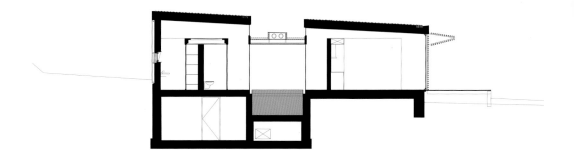

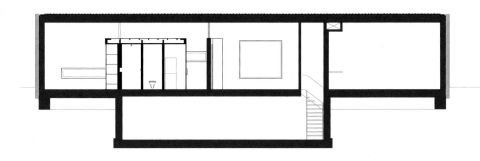

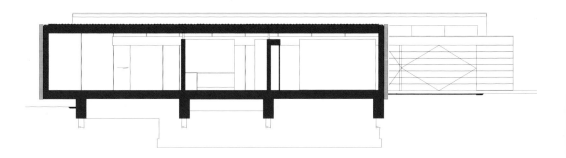

Top: Section showing the pool in the dwelling's centre.

Centre: Longitudinal section showing some of the dwelling's living areas.

Above: A section showing the garage on the right and the private quarters to the left.

The southern facade consists of sliding doors, which can be opened or closed according to weather conditions. The blinds, made of horizontal wooden slats, form a porch above the outdoor terrace.

Most of the house's appliances and fixtures can be operated electronically in order to respond to some of the challenges faced by the occupants. To avoid obstacles and to create an aesthetically pleasing effect, the control hubs are located in the basement walls and ceilings. Sliding doors, lighting and curtains have automated controls to avoid risky physical activity.

As the occupants age, it is assumed that the risk of accidents may rise. Therefore, light and colour differentiation was used in the initial design to prepare for possible deterioration of vision. And non-slip flooring around the bathroom and the kitchen was used to prevent accidents. In addition, the garage is designed to be converted into a nurse's room to house live-in help should it be needed in the future.

Top left: View into the distance from the patio.

Top right: The living area.

Bottom Left: View of the patio from the living room.

Bottom right: A passage to the outdoors equipped with an automatic door opener.

Chapter 3
MULTIGENERATIONAL LIVING

In the drive for housing innovation, it is always valuable to look to the past for inspiration. Multigenerational dwellings are just that: the reintroduction of a traditional living arrangement in response to current societal needs. In pre-industrial times, dwellings housed several generations of the same family, and even though this type of cohabitation has fallen out of favour in modern times, designers are responding to contemporary demographic shifts by recalling such concepts.

A report by the World Health Organization (WHO, 2010) suggests that the average global life expectancy rose from 64 to 68 years of age from 1990 to 2008, while fertility rates dropped from 3.3 children per woman to 2.5 in the same period. This large shift places a burden on the younger generation, who will have to support older family members while raising their own children (Population Reference Bureau 2008). Multigenerational dwellings are therefore, regarded as a possible solution for such situations.

According to Zhao (2001), 'multigenerational living occurs when a dwelling includes two or more self-contained units with certain connection'. It creates a mutual support system whereby the elderly can take part in child raising and allows the young to devote time to their careers. On the other hand, living near younger generations gives senior citizens a chance to pass on their life experience, and have a role and a sense of purpose.

When asked to design such dwellings, architects recognized that the traditional multigenerational models do not fit current needs and lifestyles due to lack of privacy. Therefore, new design concepts, that include spatial arrangements between each generation, need to be adopted (Herwig 2008). In the year 2000, the Fourth International Conference on Positive Ageing met and concluded that two major themes of multigenerational dwelling design are the encouragement of harmony and the reduction of conflict within the household. They proposed five key aspects for consideration by designers: crowding, personal independence, level of privacy, territorial issues and personal and private space. These details can be taken care of with the careful design of private versus public space.

Multigenerational dwellings require the separation of family units, so that each household can live independently should they choose to. This also makes the future sale or letting of units possible. It is also recommended that every household have its own street entrance so that members of each generation can leave and enter without disrupting the other. Indoors, it is important to distinguish between communal and individual, private areas. Communal spaces should be larger to accommodate visitors and avoid crowding. Large windows, balconies and open spaces can help in such situations. With regard to individual areas, it is important to design them so that they can be sectioned off from the communal spaces. Senior citizens, in particular, value personal space because it increases their sense of independence (Parker 2000).

Some spaces in multigenerational dwellings may require special design considerations. For example, the senior citizens' residence can be placed on the ground floor to minimize use of stairs. The space can be designed along principles of ageing in place, which were outlined in chapter 2 (see pages 22–29). In addition, units for families with children will require more bedrooms. According to cultural norms, if one generation commonly hosts social gatherings, their unit should be designed with ample communal areas. Finally, the structure should accommodate the evolving nature of all households.

There are four primary design types for multigenerational housing: garden suites, which are also known as 'granny suites', bi-family dwellings, plex units and the accessory apartment (Zhao 2001). The garden suite consists of a self-contained living unit that is positioned in the rear or side gardens of an existing house. Both dwellings can be linked by a deck or a path. The suite is designed for independent living, containing amenities such as a kitchen and bathroom. The structure may be rented or used by young adults should they choose to live with their parents later. It is also possible to link the unit to the main house. In general, this type of multigenerational dwelling is portable in nature, which allows it to be removed or relocated at a later stage.

Bi-family units and plex housing are very much alike. A bi-family unit is also called a side-by-side arrangement, while the plex is also referred to as an up-and-down design (Zhao 2001). Despite the fact that bi-family units share the same facade and side wall with the main house, they have no internal connections. Plexes exist as duplexes (two stacked units) or triplexes (three stacked units), and it is common for each unit to have its own street access. Although plexes may not have an internal connection, they can be joined via a rear staircase. Due to their spatial arrangement, both plex and bi-family units are more suitable for households with frequently evolving space needs.

The last housing type is the accessory apartment. This is typically the most integrated form of multigenerational living since a smaller apartment is usually situated within, or cornered-off from the primary living space. The two spaces can be attached, but it is recommended that each have its own direct entrance. The level of separation within the house should be designed to cater to each family's current and future needs. This type of multigenerational housing is the least adaptable for resale, rent or modification due to its inclusion in the main dwelling unit.

Multigenerational housing has seen recent change and is likely to experience more development as new technologies are invented. The German Government, for example, has recognized the value of and need for multigenerational dwellings and is creating financial plans to promote a return to large family living arrangements for economic reasons (Herwig 2008). One can therefore expect the expansion of multigenerational living as the elderly population in many nations grows.

DRIVING FORCES

- Larger number of seniors
- Increase in the cost of assisted living
- Longer life expectancy
- Desire to maintain traditional cultural values

INNOVATIONS

- Creating private spaces for each household within the single dwelling
- Prefabricated garden suites
- Conversion of garages into dwellings
- Separate street entrances for each unit

Figure 3.1: Designed by the Swiss firm Bauart, Option is a prefabricated unit that can be installed at the rear of an existing dwelling.

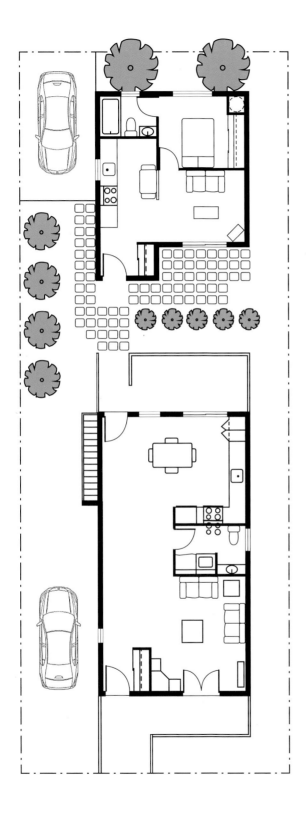

Figure 3.2: Example of a home with a rear garden suite.

3.1 MULTIGENERATIONAL LIVING

Project	Jones House
Location	Vordertau, Germany
Architect	Reinhardt Jung

Originally built in the 1960s, Jones House has gone through several renovations between 1967 and 1986. It is a dwelling for a family that spans four generations and is composed of parents, children, grandmother and great grandmother. By responding to societal changes and the needs of this ever-changing family, architects Reinhardt Jung wisely integrated the various parts of the house and the needs of its occupants. By using contemporary design principles and preserving traditional values, the designers ensured that the occupants have their own privacy while sharing space.

The house measures 116 m^2 (1,249 s ft), and each generation has its own suite of bedrooms and other private spaces on the different levels of its three-storeys. For accessibility reasons, the grandmother and great

Below: Rear elevation at night showing the addition.

Below: First floor plan showing the
upper unit.

Right: Ground floor and rear yard.
The location of the stairs permits simple
access to the upper unit.

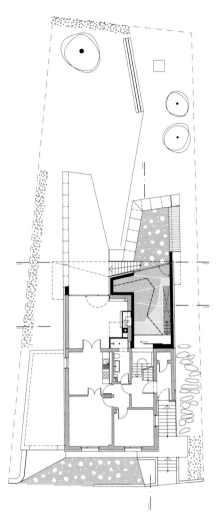

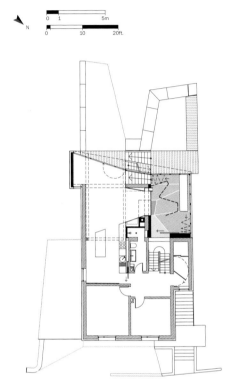

Left: Street facade with
neighbouring dwellings.

grandmother have their rooms on the ground floor. By examining the house's section, you can see the original three-storey dwelling, and that the enlarged living spaces create a further interaction between the floors. Also, the living room, dining room and outdoor terrace surround a central fireplace that adds to a communal feeling.

The new two-floor addition makes the house a five-storey, split-level, thereby increasing accessibility from one floor to the next and giving opportunities for the elderly to rest. The designer's decision to preserve architectural details such as the railings and the original wallpaper provide a constant reminder of the house's history, while the floor-to-ceiling windows provide a view of its surroundings. These visual cues and design references help the family to move from one space to another with ease. The lowest level serves as a playroom for the children and an office for their parents. The well-designed spaces allow the various generations to have distinct areas of their own with minimal disturbance.

Below: Sections showing the old structure and the new addition.

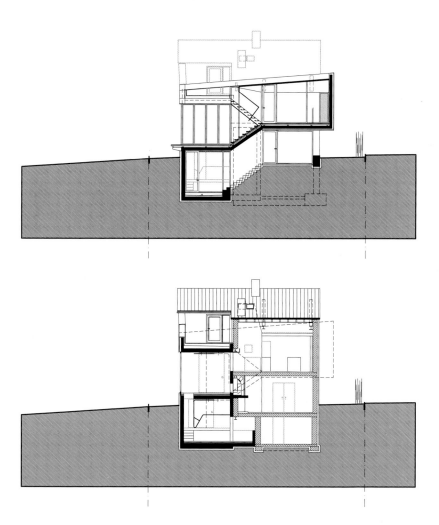

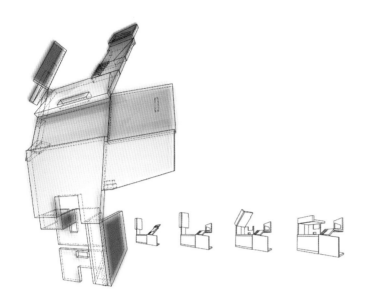

Top: Computer-generated fold and the series of spaces.

Above left: View of the living area.

Left: The patio area with a view of the office.

3.2 MULTIGENERATIONAL LIVING

Project   Ravine House
Location   Toronto, Ontario, Canada
Architect   Cindy Rendely Architexture

Architect Cindy Rendely designed an award-winning house for her clients, a couple with three teenaged sons who live with the elderly parents of one of the household's heads. Situated in Toronto, Canada, the house is harmonized with the nearby ravine by including large windows and openings. The architect paid attention to communal family living, while at the same time satisfying a need for privacy for every generation. Considering the number of households it encompasses, the 632 m² (6,800 sq ft) house exhibits both efficiency and functionality.

The house has three floors. The entrance is on the ground level and stone stairs that parallel the rising topography of the environment lead the way up to the house. The couple and their teenaged children have their own bedrooms and private spaces on

Above: Rear view at nighttime showing the space between the two structures.

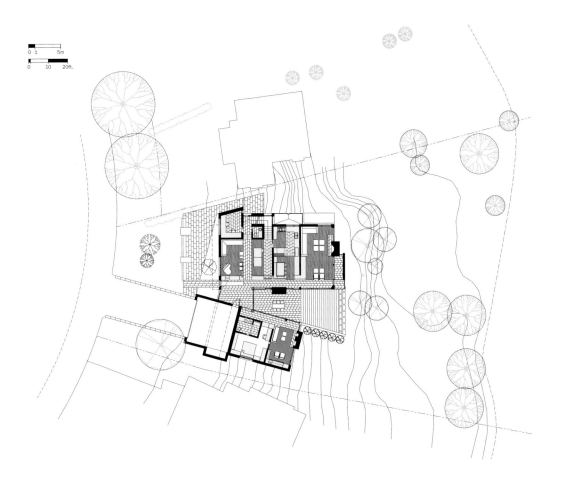

Above: Site and ground floor plans showing the main house and the one for the parents.

Left: A view of the hallway and the dining room.

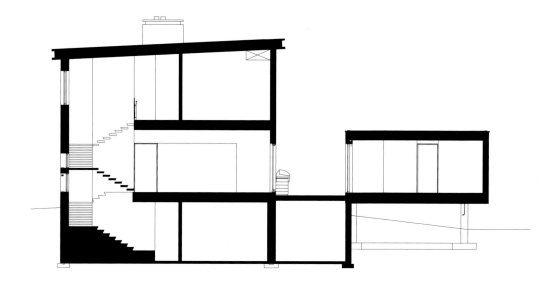

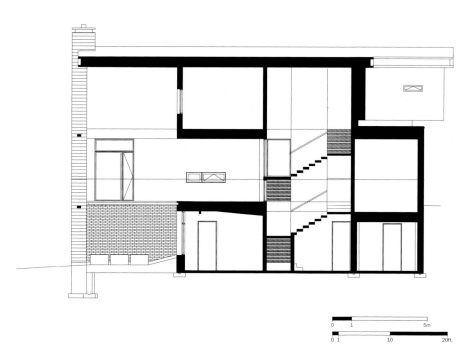

Top: A section showing the space
between the two structures.

Above: Cross-section showing the two
storey living area.

the upper floor.

The elderly occupants of the house have their own apartments. Rendely wanted to give them highly accessible and safe spaces. The ground floor contains no stairs; it has pocket doors instead of swinging doors, a 1.5 m (5 ft) turnaround radius in the bathroom, guardrails and colourful furniture and flooring. The apartment provides visual and acoustic privacy from the main floor. The living area on the ground floor allows the family

to gather and socialize. A few fireplaces made from natural stone in the living area also provide opportunities for family get-togethers. The lower floor is an entertainment area where the teenagers can invite their friends.

The dwelling was designed with floor-to-ceiling windows to allow its occupants to appreciate the surrounding scenery during all seasons. The intricate details and choice of materials present a minimalist interior finish that employs a playful balance

between the exterior stone facade and the landscape of the ravine. The hardwood floors aid the mobility of the elderly members of the family as well as integrating the dwelling with the surrounding natural landscape.

Above: View of the patio and the living area.

Top right: Interior view of the living area.

Above right: View of the outside patio from the interior.

Chapter 4
SMALL HOMES

Rising housing and heating costs, the emergence of the non-traditional small household and an increase in the number of senior citizens have all contributed to a renewed interest in small-sized dwellings (Burney 2010). Small dwellings can arbitrarily be defined as those with a floor area not exceeding 56 m² (500 sq ft). They are already common in crowded European and Asian cities, yet their popularity has been rising rapidly in other parts of the world following the 2008 economic meltdown (Burney 2010). Consumers are becoming aware of the environmental and budgetary implications of owning a very large single-family home, especially when some spaces in these homes are hardly used (Kurutz 2008). Other notable advantages of small homes are lower property taxes and construction costs, time saving through the possibility of prefabrication and lower

Figure 4.1: Design strategies to enhance the perception of space in a small house.

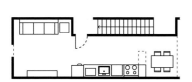

Open plan and a minimum of partitions allows a space to appear larger.

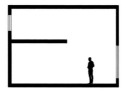

Changes in room height, length or width delimit spaces without need for partitions.

Steps and level changes underscore spatial and functional transitions.

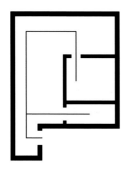

Well-conceived circulation through rooms eliminates the need for passageways.

Pocket doors and doors that open outwards facilitate and reduce circulation space.

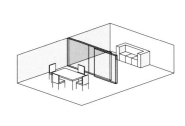

Sliding partitions or transparent materials make spaces appear larger.

maintenance fees (Losantos 2006, Morcos 2009, Gutierrez 2008).

To be efficient, small dwellings must be carefully designed because minor decisions can have a large impact. Also, the reduced space can put occupants in close proximity to each other and a feeling of crowding can ensue. Light, boundaries, circulation, choice of materials and furnishings should all be considered by designers and used to resolve challenges and expand spatial perception. A good design should not only be versatile and efficient, but also avoid simplicity and dullness.

One of the strategies employed to improve the perception of space in a small house is to increase natural light through proper placement of windows (Morcos 2009). In rural settings the house may have large openings to the landscape on all elevations. In urban areas, however, privacy and property regulations present

Figure 4.2: Interior design strategies to maximize use of space in a small house.

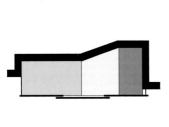

Concealing irregular spaces behind panel-doors enhances linearity and spaciousness.

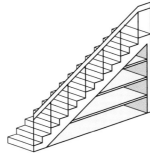

Storage spaces can take advantage of residual spaces, under stairs, in niches, between beams.

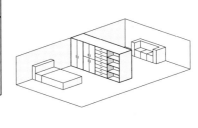

Large storage units can function as room dividers and partitions.

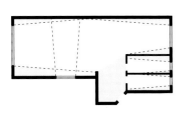

Different window sizes and orientations bring in varying quantities of natural light and increase the quality of the interior space.

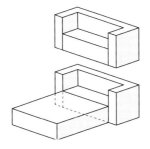

Multifunctional furniture increases spatial efficiency.

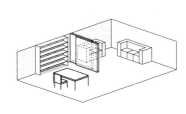

Multifunctional rooms and transformable spaces increase the usability of a space.

a unique challenge to designers who have to negotiate the division between public and private spaces. Some architects, such as Ban, Takaharu and Yui have pioneered solutions to these problems by using curtains or shutters to separate the outdoors and the indoors (Ban 2011, Takaharu and Yui 2011a, Takaharu and Yui 2011b). Such fixtures can be opened during the day to let in light and fresh air, but can be closed at night. Those designers also encourage the inhabitants to engage with the outside by creating large, easily accessible rooftop spaces that can be used for outdoor seating, for example.

Artificial light can also play a role in improving the perception of a small dwelling. During the night-time, it can be used to define spaces and create more flexible interior arrangements. For example, a well-lit stairwell can offer a contrast to a dark living area; thereby creating a unique experience when one enters and leaves. Also, directing light onto works of art can prevent indoor monotony (Chan 2007). Some designers also favour the reaction of light hitting white walls. Since white walls can reflect the hues of whatever light strikes them, they have the ability to make the home seem larger than it really is.

Natural light can be used to create a distinct character in a building through its interplay with materials, textures and colours, which can break up boxy rooms or help spaces flow into each other (Chan 2007). Therefore, these light–material reactions can be artfully employed to create a diverse interior character, which expands the perceptual depth of a home beyond its actual size.

Interior arrangement is an important aspect of the designer's job. Partitions and walls tend to enclose a space while open floor plans increase its use and the spatial effect (Morcos 2009, Chan 2007, Burney 2010). Therefore, a spatial overlap between different functions can reduce the need for single-purpose spaces, such as hallways, and create a floor plan in which spaces flow into each other and can be used as multipurpose areas. This can increase the space's versatility and efficiency. Open floor plans also allow light from windows to travel freely throughout the house.

When partitions must be installed, transparent ones are recommended since they still permit the dispersal of light. Moveable partitions, or sliding panels, are also useful in defining spaces because they allow small spaces to be temporarily redefined according to need. Lastly, an open floor concept with large exterior openings permits views of the outside, which, as previously noted, can increase the perception of a house's size. Increasing the floor height can greatly expand space without enlarging the floor area (Burney 2010).

Well-conceived circulation concepts are a key tool used by designers in small homes. The location of the stairs must be carefully considered since they have the potential to waste large amounts of space or block important views if misplaced.

Therefore, the material from which they're built, their style and their colour must be carefully chosen. Designers often select 'minimal stairs', using cantilevered boards or spiral staircases, to maximize space and avoid visual clutter.

To define spaces without cluttering them, designers can use built-in storage. A sizeable amount of space is commonly taken up by 'stuff', such as seldom-used furniture and single-purpose items. Since having storage in a small house is critical, designers can create hidden storage in walls or under beds. Some designers have introduced dish closets and clothes racks in the ceiling, which descend with a gentle push (Consexto Architects 2010). Furniture can be made more space efficient by embedding it into the structure (Chan 2007). Beds and fixtures can be folded into the walls when not in use. Furthermore, items can have multiple uses, rather than a single one. Shower heads can, for example, be swivelled to become kitchen sink taps if needed and storage cabinets can be double sided (Loftcube 2006). When designed properly, built-ins can reduce clutter without compromising functional aspects.

Small home designs have made large advances and have further potential as technology improves. Their proliferation holds several societal advantages, such as offering affordable housing solutions and reducing environmental footprints.

DRIVING FORCES

- Economic downturn
- Rising housing and heating costs
- Emergence of non-traditional households
- Environmental awareness

INNOVATIONS

- Manipulation of natural and artificial light
- Linking indoor/outdoor space
- Interior arrangement using panels/partitions
- Multiple-use areas
- Storage solutions

4.1 SMALL HOMES

Project	L41 Home
Location	Vancouver, British Columbia, Canada
Architect	Michael Katz, Architect, and Janet Crone, Designer

The L41 home, designed by Vancouver architect Michael Katz and designer Janet Crone embodies the idea that one can enjoy life in a home of only 23 m² (250 sq ft). The thrust of the design is to create an affordable and livable home in a small space.

Every interior space is cleverly designed. There are no swinging doors to taint the clean walls or add unnecessary obstacles. With a convertible living–bedroom space, the occupant can store unused furniture, such as a bed, computer desk, cabinets or drawers in the walls. One of the featured examples of this is a pull-down blind behind the couch that can be converted into a projection screen. In contrast to ultra-small or micro-homes, L41's kitchen is U-shaped and of a regular size, allowing the occupant to prepare meals comfortably.

The L41 home was designed to appeal to diverse groups. Similar to Ford's Model T car, the architects intended to provide an affordable product. With this

Below: Rear view showing the convertible living-bedroom space.

Top: The principal entrance to the unit.

Middle: View of the efficiently-designed kitchen.

Bottom: View of the living-bedroom area.

in mind, the design of the units is modular and can be expanded or customized based on clients' needs. Furthermore, the houses can be configured to become a single unit or an entire apartment complex.

Environmentally aware and appreciative of the impact of mass production, the architects designed the house with engineered, cross-laminated timber made from beetle-killed pine trees and structurally sturdy modules that can be used singly or stacked together to form a mid-rise building. Concerns for energy and resource efficiency were also a key factor. Green technologies such as LED lighting, green roofs, heat recovery ventilation and solar heating not only ameliorate the occupants' living carbon footprint, but also educate the community about the environment.

Above: View of the bathroom with the shower stall.

Top: Computer render of a two-storey unit.

Middle: Computer render of a wide span unit.

Bottom: Computer render of a cluster made up of L41 homes.

4.2 SMALL HOMES

Project   House to Catch the Forest
Location   Chini Shi, Nagano, Japan
Architect   Tezuka Architects

Located in the forests of Chino, Nagano, Japan, the House to Catch the Forest is elevated by concrete walls above gradually descending terrain. The one-storey house is sited in the middle of a red pine forest and the facade mimics the dark-toned tree trunks integrating the dwelling with its surroundings. The house has an area of 81 m² (872 sq ft) and the designers increased the angled roof height to suit the purpose of each interior space.

The architects placed the stairways near the exterior wall to reduce any unused space and visual obstacles. The open-plan eliminated the need for wall dividers and transitional corridors. Instead, washrooms and closets are positioned to foster privacy between the living and sleeping spaces. Two floor-to-ceiling

windows flank the house. This design feature offers a pristine view of the forest from both facades. Doors at the ends of the large windows lead the occupants to the open balcony, which is protected by the overhanging roof, further connecting them with their environment.

The interior design is minimal. The elimination of doors creates an open-plan flow and reduces visual obstructions. The expanded ceiling space over the living area and the resultant mass light permeation makes the space feel large and pleasant. Additional openings around the house, such as a skylight and the stairs, also provide flexible physical and visual connections with nature.

Below: Section through the site showing the proximity of the house and the forest.

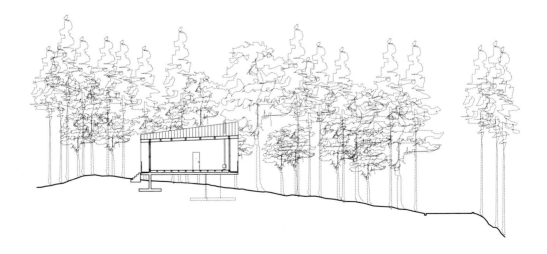

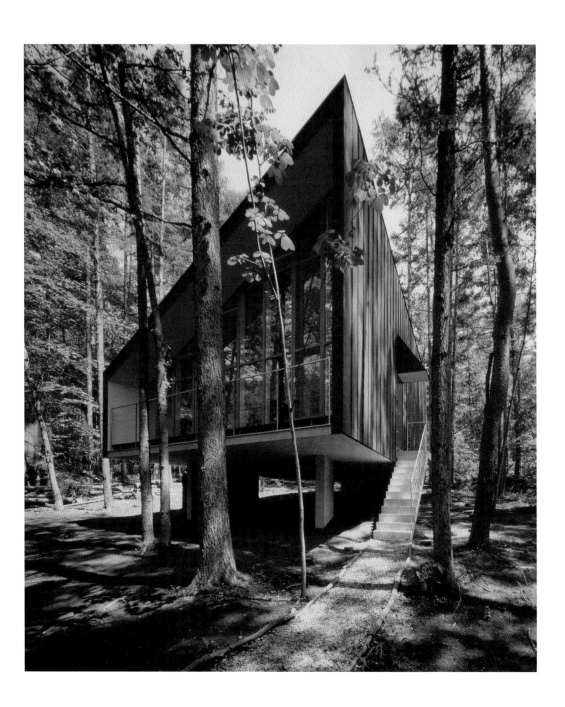

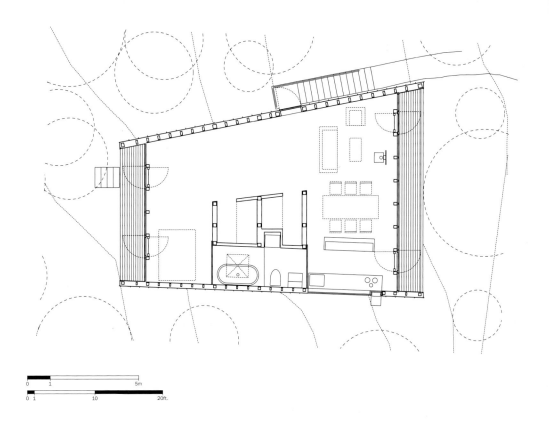

Above: Floor plan showing the highly efficient use of the small space.

Left: Perspective section through the kitchen area.

Opposite page top: View of the living-dining areas.

Opposite page bottom: The openness is well represented in this photo of the living-dining areas.

Economic difficulties have taken their toll on society, affecting world markets and the lives of individual citizens. Secure employment and steady incomes are becoming less common, which makes it highly difficult for first-time buyers to purchase homes in the world's highly populated urban centres. In addition, an affordability gap has emerged, where the rate of increase of housing prices has surpassed the rate of rise in household incomes.

Whereas in the past buyers sought large homes, which often overstretched their financial limits, following the 2008 global real estate meltdown, a different mindset has begun to dominate. A growing number of would-be homeowners can no longer accumulate the financial means necessary to buy a home and, as a consequence, the demand for less expensive, smaller and more energy-efficient homes is rising.

Demographic transformations and the rise of non-traditional households are also likely to increase the market share of small housing units. The need to consider new design concepts, and production methods that address these fundamental changes is evident. Adaptable and expandable designs, prefabricated and narrow units are some of the concepts that will be explored in this section.

Chapter 5
ADAPTABLE HOUSES

With increasing numbers of non-traditional households – including singles and single parents – limited, conventionally designed housing layouts no longer suit the needs of all potential occupants. In addition, an increasingly elderly population has created a demand for dwellings that can be adapted to the evolving lives of their occupants without requiring costly and intensive alterations (Palmer and Ward 2010).

Adaptable units accommodate varying spatial needs and facilitate the introduction of new building systems without compromising functionality or comfort. These homes use design concepts and technologies to create an environment in which modifying the building is preferable and more readily achievable than moving to a new location or demolition. While fully adaptable houses include aging in place and expandable homes principles, this chapter only focuses on adaptability.

For a house to be adaptable, it is important to design layouts that can be flexible to the needs of the household as it changes. This involves macro considerations, such as the design of the overall structure to provide adaptable interiors, and micro considerations, like the positioning of doors and wet functions (kitchens and bathrooms).

One way to have a flexible layout is to design a structure that requires little or no internal load-bearing support (Friedman 2002). This can be done either by designing a narrow house with floor joists that span the entire space between the two exterior longitudinal walls or by using products such as I- or open-web wooden joists, which allow greater spanning distances. Creating large, open floor spaces permits maximum adaptability.

If the structure does require internal supports, it is important to place them adjacent to permanent functions, such as the bathroom and the kitchen, which are unlikely to be moved. Wet functions, however, which are difficult and expensive to relocate, should be grouped together and placed between zones.

Once a large, uninterrupted floor has been constructed, the space itself must also be arranged for maximum adaptability; creating an open floor plan with multipurpose uses can achieve this. A successful multipurpose space can be designed with dimensions and proportions to accommodate a variety of activities such as sleeping, sitting or working. These spaces need to be as large and as square as possible to expand adaptability options. Room sizes of 3.7 by 3.7 m (12

by 12 ft) up to 4.6 by 4.6 m (15 by 15 ft) should be sufficient to accommodate any future adaptations (Friedman 2002). In addition, it is important that these multipurpose spaces contain no defining features, like closets, which tend to limit their overall adaptability.

For each of these multipurpose spaces, the placement of doors should be made to allow further adaptability. Doors located near the corners of a room, for example, permit the space to be divided in two because another door can easily be added elsewhere when needed. This arrangement also increases efficiency because it does not interrupt circulation. Furthermore, if the door is placed in the corner it makes more sense to leave a small gap for shallow storage along the wall behind it.

Another consideration of adaptable design is creating housing with effective integrative circulation. Initially, this means avoiding building in paths that pass through the middle of spaces, which tends to designate them as public and prevents their future conversion into private rooms without considerable alterations. Creating an independent path that feeds into the living spaces is the best option. These can be located either along a wall, or in a central place from which other multipurpose spaces are reached. It is also important that these paths are treated as multifunctional spaces, in order to increase their efficiency and ultimately their potential adaptability. This can involve widening halls and incorporating features such as temporary storage along their walls. If an extension is built in

Figure 5.1 The use of I-joists as structural members allows for greater spanning distances, which eliminates the need for loadbearing walls and offers interior adaptability.

future, these storage areas can easily and affordably be removed and replaced with stairs. Positioning stairs as a wedge facing the middle of a floor should be avoided since it creates a large central space that cannot be used or adapted easily.

After such decisions have been made, residual spaces might be left. These consist of areas under the stairs, or the small alcoves in bay windows or corridors, which are good locations for storage and allow for greater adaptability within the larger areas.

Beyond circulation and flexible layouts, the use of adaptable utilities or service modules is another way to increase adaptability. This involves using items such as movable kitchen cabinets, or modular furniture components, which can easily be rearranged. It is also possible to use furniture for the division of spaces; storage, such as shelves, can be used to distinguish different functional areas within a large room.

In parallel, designing utilities for adaptability is vital in adaptable dwellings. Plumbing, ventilation and heating systems require maintenance and updating due to technological advancements and general wear-and-tear. Therefore, it is essential that these systems be easily accessible should they malfunction or require updating. This can be done by including a vertical service shaft with accessible chases. A chase is a horizontal tube that runs in each floor and contains the essential utilities needed for that floor. A vertical service shaft may originate at the mechanical rooms and bring all conduits up to allow them to break off into sub-chases at each floor as needed. The chase could be accessible through a floor panel for easy reach by service professionals without causing major damage to existing walls or floors (Friedman 2002).

It is also possible to use an accessible feeder pipe for electrical outlets. In multipurpose spaces, outlets must be placed either along the walls or within the floor due to the fact that building

Figure 5.2 Placing a door near the corner of a room and having two windows will facilitate division of that room in two.

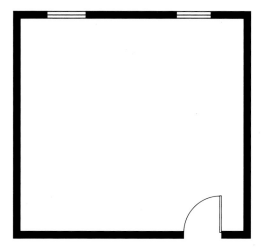 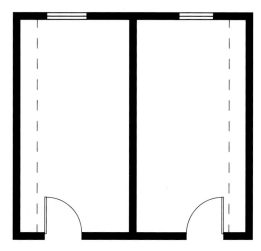

regulations prohibit their placement in demountable partitions. This allows homeowners to use matrix tiles and baseboard profiles as feeder tubes for electric wires and cables, which in turn allows for greater adaptability, as computer stations and phone jacks are no longer limited by traditional wall outlets. This idea can even be extended to the kitchen, where electrical raceways can be placed along counters to allow the hook-up of appliances anywhere.

When one recognizes the many benefits of adaptable housing, it becomes clear why such designs are starting to be accepted by the industry and governments. The Australian Government, for instance, has already specified strict codes for not only adaptable housing, but also accessible and universal housing designs (Palmer and Ward 2010).

DRIVING FORCES

- Rise in the number of non-traditional households
- Lack of innovatively designed interiors
- High cost of housing
- New technological advances

INNOVATIONS

- Demountable partitions
- Flexible plumbing fixtures and fittings
- Multi-purpose space design
- Thoughtful placement of doors
- Use of moveable cabinets

5.1 ADAPTABLE HOUSES

Project	Butler House
Location	Melbourne, Australia
Architect	Andrew Maynard Architects

The Butler House is an elegant warehouse-turned-residence designed by the Australian firm Andrew Maynard Architects. The client, a household with two young boys, asked for a livable and adaptable house based on the present and future needs of each member. The original warehouse measured 44 m^2 (474 sq ft), lacked sound and thermal insulation, had minimal infiltration of natural light, and lacked space and privacy.

The architect solved these challenges by removing the existing roof, and replacing it with a canopy-covered terrace. The addition of the 85 m^2 (915 sq ft) terrace introduced a quality that many houses in the city lack: an outdoor private area adequate for family gatherings. A skylight floods the three floors with natural light that also ties the levels together. Adjustable louvres and timber shelves can be used as bookshelves, but also as spatially functional slides to control acoustic level and light infiltration. In the summer, a passive solar design approach

Below: The rooftop outdoor area with the adjustable louvres.

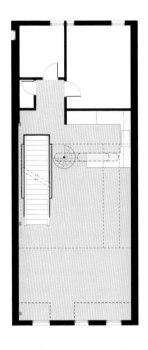

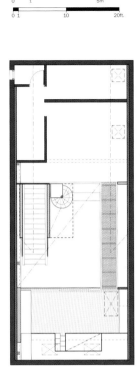

Top: Ground (left), second floor (middle) and upper level (right) in an open design concept.

Above left: A view of the living room from the mezzanine.

Above right: The open stair represents the adaptability of the dwelling.

protects the roof terrace from direct sunlight exposure and rain, while opened louvres allow light, sound and ventilation to travel through the house.

The children's rooms are located on the mezzanine. The rooms are protected by a sliding wall that offers privacy control and noise protection when needed. The strategic placement of the beds, desk and storage leaves room for additional furniture, such as a double bed, if needed for visiting family members. Similarly, on the other side of the same floor, the master bedroom also has a large sliding door. By using adjustable design features, the Butler House offers private and collective spaces for all family members and their guests.

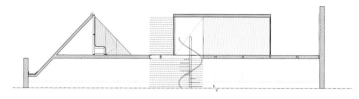

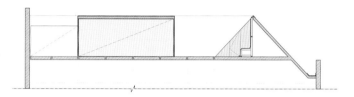

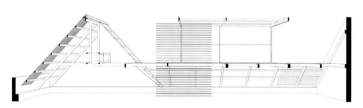

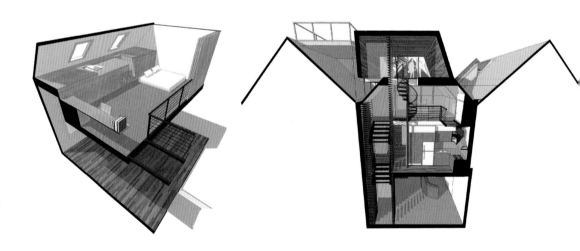

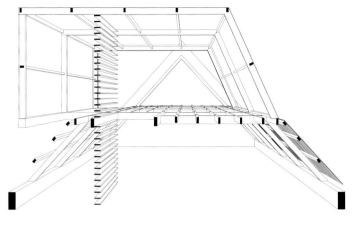

Top: Perspective showing the roof structure.

Centre: Perspective showing the new roof addition.

Below: A longitudinal section illustrating the open spaces of the home.

Opposite page, top: Section showing the old and the newly added roofs.

Opposite page, bottom: Cross sections showing all floors.

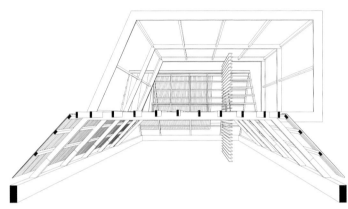

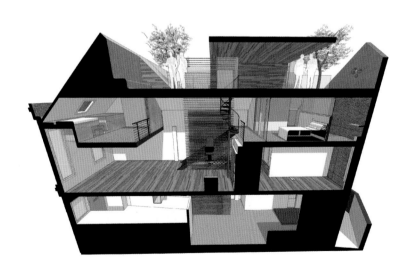

5.2 ADAPTABLE HOUSES

Project	Live Work Home
Location	Syracuse, New York, USA
Architect	Cook + Fox Architects

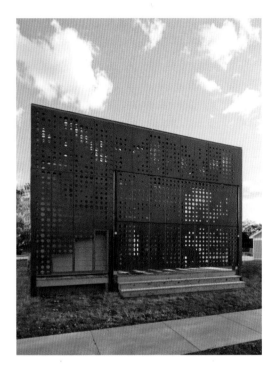 

Located in Near West Side, Syracuse, New York, the firm Cook+Fox Architects took careful note of their economically deprived neighbourhood when designing the Live Work Home, looking at both its current situation and future potential. The architects' idea was to mix residential and commercial activities in one building to generate new opportunities. The resulting home, which measures 126 m^2 (1360 sq ft), is an addition to a community that is comprised of several family generations and age groups, as well as offices and workshops. At one storey tall, the house has ground-level access and its inherent construction qualities allow it to be expanded or reduced linearly within its given lot, according to the changing needs of its dwellers.

The design is driven by efficiency and the simple idea of adapting the interior layout through seven potential lifecycle stages, ranging from childhood to multigenerational living. The construction is achieved through a mix of prefabrication and on-site techniques and the materials used are designed for maximum

Above: Rear facade with the screen closed (left) and open (right).

Opposite page: Ground floor plan (top) demonstrates the linearity of the dwelling. Site plan (bottom).

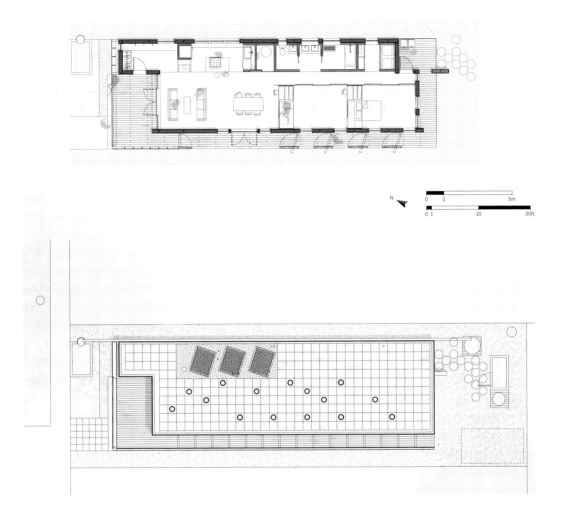

efficiency. The unique facade has an interchangeable screen that allows the family to alter the interior according to privacy and orientation preferences.

The wet areas, such as the kitchen and bathroom, are located at the core of the long plan. This allows for better accessibility for future extensions with minimal changes to the existing partitions. When the family grows, another bedroom can be added beside the existing ones. The reverse is also possible, if the family size decreases. A modular system of mobile furniture can be shifted, added to or removed to reduce unused space and meet the demands of household members. These design features are significant when contrasted with the costly renovations associated with non-adaptable units. The furniture and the prefabricated wall partitions also offer opportunities for do-it-yourself remodelling.

In an effort to achieve LEED certification, the architects employed several 'green' technologies when constructing the house. Energy consumption is reduced with the use of solar panels and a geothermal heating system, while the strategic north-south openings allow for cross-ventilation and also allow heat recovery ventilators (HRV) to constantly filter indoor air. Aiming to revitalize the community, Cook + Fox Architects are hopeful that the Live Work Home, used as a prototype for future building, will sustain and serve a wide range of family types and economic needs.

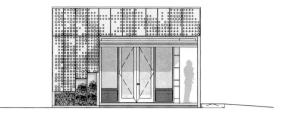

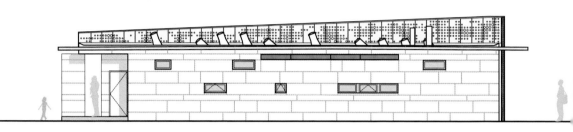

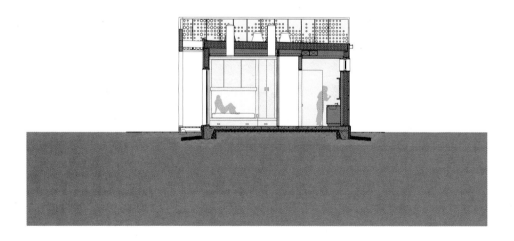

Top: Rear elevation with the folded screen.

Middle: Side elevation showing point of light penetration through the roof.

Above: Section showing the dwelling's rectangular shape.

Above left and right: Screens allow
the space to be divided, but clever use
of latticework prevents the areas from
seeming dark.

Chapter 6
GROWING HOMES

Expandable dwellings, also known as 'grow homes', are purposely designed to allow occupants to increase their living space either internally or externally. As a result, homeowners are able to reside in the same location for longer rather than move, and to foster a stronger sense of community, where inhabitants know each other and invest in their locale. This idea is applicable to all households, but in particular to young first-time homebuyers and empty nesters who may experience frequent changes during some of their life stages (CMHC 2011a). Its success is largely due to the fact that expandable homes are not only more affordable, but also tie in to the larger do-it-yourself (DIY) trend. The two main methods of creating expandable dwellings, 'add-on' and 'add-in' are discussed in this chapter.

Figure 6.1: Methods of implementing add-in areas in a dwelling.

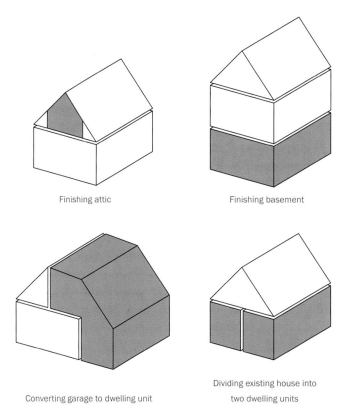

Finishing attic

Finishing basement

Converting garage to dwelling unit

Dividing existing house into two dwelling units

An add-on design is centred on the idea of expansion through addition. These small homes are designed to be added-on to. Decisions made in their initial design are crucial since hallways, interior spaces and facades must be made to work with any future additions. While expanding in a rural setting is generally easy due to larger lots, adding in urban locations must be carefully planned because of the limited space. For horizontal expansion, through ground level additions, it is important to allocate adequate outdoor space in the initial designs. It is also necessary to ensure that the planned additions will not exceed municipal bylaw limits regarding lot coverage and setbacks (Sullivan 2011).

It is also possible to expand vertically, either by adding floors on top of an existing structure, or in an extreme case, by

Figure 6.2: Methods of implementing add-on areas in a dwelling.

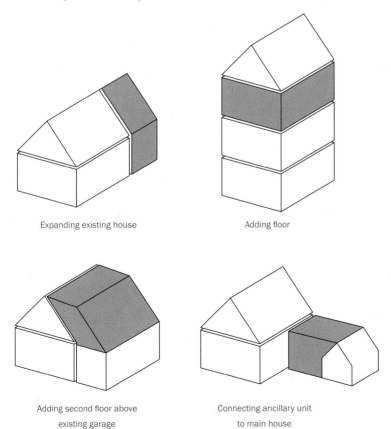

Expanding existing house

Adding floor

Adding second floor above
existing garage

Connecting ancillary unit
to main house

adding a lower floor by raising the building. For both options, it is important to incorporate appropriate structural considerations in the initial design to avoid expensive adaptations. Designers of future additions, whether they are horizontal or vertical, should also consider the larger urban context, the surrounding buildings and their occupants' views, for example (Friedman 2001).

For exterior features, such as facade and roof contours, it is important, in the initial design phase, to use wall heights and materials that can easily be added-on to. It is also necessary to design so that the envisaged addition will remain visually proportionate to the original unit (Garnett 2011). For site planning, it is also recommended that factors such as natural drainage, local vegetation and trees will not altered by such additions.

Internally, the initial circulation arrangement becomes a major contributing factor to the success of the expansion. Having the main hallway of the existing structure reach an exterior wall, for example, allows for its extension without creating unwanted secondary movement through rooms (Garnett 2011). Initial plans must also arrange for alternative circulation to minimize disturbance during the construction. In general, having a detailed plan of future additions will allow designers and homeowners to anticipate and prevent any difficulty with aesthetics, functionality and circulation.

Another advantage of add-on homes is the possibility of having the addition prefabricated and shipped to the site. This approach negates issues with vandalism, material storage and weather delays, and ensures less interruption of daily family routines, due to time saved during on-site construction. The add-on method also means that the homeowner is not paying for heating and maintenance of unused spaces (Sullivan 2011). By only adding spaces when they are required, a homeowner stands to save resources by not having to maintain extra space. The downside to the add-on method, however, is the larger cost associated with adding space and renovating. Rather than simply adding interior walls – as with the add-in method – one must build on-site, or prefabricate an addition (Sullivan 2011).

The second type of expandable homes are those that follow the add-in method. This involves initially constructing a larger, partially complete shell to allow for incremental growth. In the first phase, only the primary living spaces are built, leaving vacant, unfinished areas to be completed as and when the owner needs them. The advantage of this approach is the lower cost of finishing an area rather than building it anew, and the possibility of the owners doing the work themselves.

Much like expandable homes, add-in homes require initial consideration regarding the potential direction of expansion. For these housing types, vertical expansion tends to be the most common and sensible option. This means that the ground level is finished during the initial phase, leaving the first floor, attic or basement to be completed later. Designers may choose to put large windows and standard ceiling heights in these places to facilitate their later expansion. Another good option is locating unfinished areas away from finished ones to prevent any unsightly interference between them. This separation also allows the owner to finish the house without interrupting daily routines (CMHC 2011a).

The Grow Home, originally designed and built at McGill University in Montreal, Canada, is a good example of an add-in strategy. Winner of the 1999 World Habitat Award, the design is an affordable, narrow home that was constructed with an un-partitioned second floor. It was adopted by the homebuilding industry as quality, affordable housing for first-time homebuyers (Friedman 2001).

Designing for flexibility is essential in all types of expandable homes since it aims to provide an easy way of re-designating spaces and building on additions. Primarily, it includes selecting suitable structural components and wall materials. Wooden stud walls covered with gypsum, for example, can easily be punctured to create a doorway to an addition. Also, demountable interior partitions are easier to manipulate when changes are needed.

Locating wet functions, such as bathrooms and kitchens, centrally allows for the addition of rooms without changes to plumbing lines and fixtures. Also, rooms with non-permanent fixtures allow homeowners to re-designate the function of a room without the need for large-scale alterations (Sullivan 2011). This room-function flexibility gives homeowners the option to use both add-on and add-in expansion methods.

For room function changes, however, it is important to initially plan for and install utilities for the future introduction of additional plumbing, electricity and appliances. Central heating, for example, reduces the duct work needed. Also, extending plumbing work to potential future bathroom sites prevents major changes to the primary structure during construction. Both of these examples can succeed in reducing labour-intensive procedures and costs at a later date.

While both add-in and add-on homes have their own unique characteristics, homeowners often mix both methods to create dwellings that are customized. This supports the notion that a house should accommodate the occupants, rather than the occupants adjusting their needs to the dwelling's constraints.

DRIVING FORCES

- High cost of housing
- New household types
- Increase in DIY skills
- Technological advances, including new materials

INNOVATIONS

- Advances in prefabrication
- Flexible fittings and plumbing
- Wide-spanning floor joists
- Development of demountable partitions

6.1 GROWING HOMES

Project	MOMO – Modern Modular
Location	Öland, Sweden
Architect	Grasshopper AB

For the Swedish architectural studio Grasshopper, the MOMO house is a dwelling that represents a framework for life. The house is a modern interpretation of the fast-paced, changing lifestyles of families. For instance, it can be used by households as a weekend getaway cottage, as well as accommodating the constantly evolving needs of young couples. Without a need for heavy construction, the architects' intention was to achieve fast-paced assembly when changing the house, both in size and design. Using prefabricated techniques, modules measuring 10 m^2 (107 sq ft) are placed next to each other in a variety of configurations, ultimately based on the homeowner's preference for privacy, spatial separation and family size. The larger module contains the living room, bedroom, bathroom and kitchen, while the smaller one is used as a guest bedroom. The open terrace between the modules implies a separation between owner and guests, or parents and children, and introduces an outdoor platform for communal experience. The sail-like membrane that acts as a protection for the terrace is a great complement to the formal, modular qualities of the house and, supported by four pillars that are attached directly to the terrain, the canvas roof can be adapted just as easily.

Bathrooms and storage are arranged between the living room and bedroom areas. In smaller-sized homes, strategic placement of this kind can help the designer to avoid unnecessary interior partitions. It also allows for easy expansion of bedroom space if the family grows, with no need to alter other parts of the house.

The modules are made of solid wooden planks and assembled in a factory. The structure sits on a wooden base held by pillars that allows for an easy relocation of the house. Furthermore, spatial flexibility and an interior–exterior relationship is generated through a selection of 13 different exterior panels and five interior partitions, while still revealing its white wooden spaces.

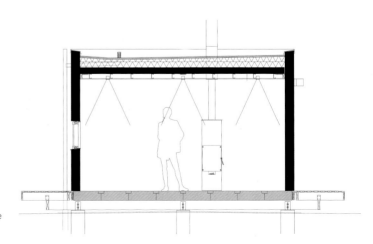

Right: A cross-section demonstrating the modular nature of the design.

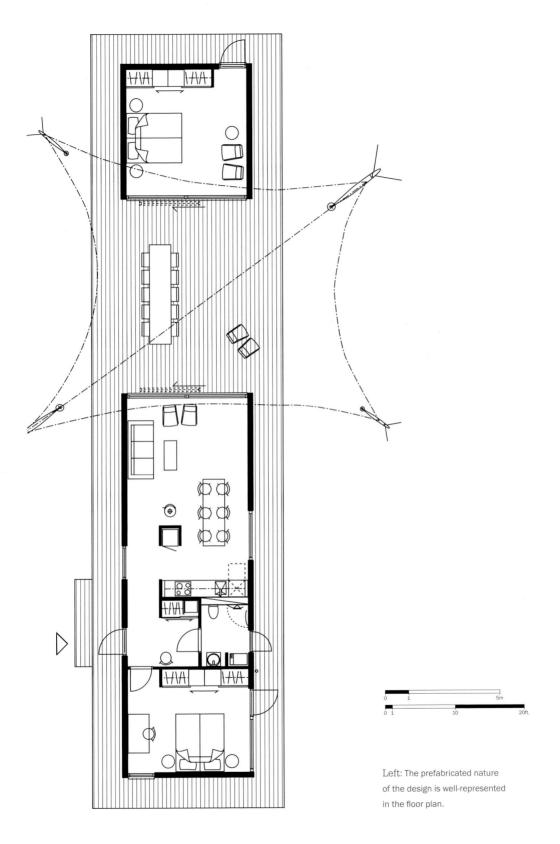

Left: The prefabricated nature
of the design is well-represented
in the floor plan.

Above: Perspective of the dwelling's two structures and the sail-covered area in between.

Opposite page, top: View from the rear bedroom.

Opposite page, bottom: A view from the living room into the small rear structure.

6.2 GROWING HOMES

Project | Prefab Lighthouses
Location | Groningen, The Netherlands
Architect | DAAD Architecten

Due to the rise of urban living, the demand for high-density dwellings in cities has increased. As a result, prices of apartments soar as developers compete for the increasingly hard-to-find land. The Dutch design firm DAAD Architecten tackled this societal issue by exploring an untapped urban landscape: the rooftops. Their project, Lighthouses, is an attempt to solve living congestion in urban areas.

Although the idea to build on rooftops is not new, DAAD's Prefab Lighthouses are an innovative and practical structural extension that uses principles of prefabrication. Each measuring approximately 6 by 4 by 3 m (20 by 13 by 10 ft), these modules can be placed on any existing building, within zoning regulations, such as apartment buildings, commercial structures and schools. Similar to plug and play construction, Prefab Lighthouses can be erected within a day or two and removed later if desired.

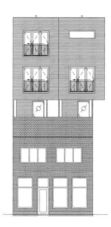

Top: Front and side elevation of the Lighthouse, which illustrates its modularity.

Above: Cross-section through the structure.

Opposite page
Top left: Installing a module

Top right: A unit with installed modules.

Below: Entrance to one of the dwellings.

The lighthouse is a residential option suitable for a variety of potential dwellers. The pieces are prefabricated in a plant and delivered to the site as a built module. The details and connections have been standardized and designed to make on-site construction simple and fast. Homeowners range from landlords, who seek additional living spaces in their residential complexes, to business owners who wish to live in the inner city and avoid the everyday commute. Lighthouse single-family units consist of three floors with an area of 41 m² (439 sq ft) created by three stacked modules standing just under 9 m (30 ft) in height. The living room and kitchen are on the first floor, while the bedrooms and studies are on the second and the third; however, based on the owner's wishes, this arrangement can be altered or even reversed.

In order to maximize (and take advantage of) the diversity of locations in which Lighthouses can be situated, doors and windows can be selected and positioned at four different locations in the module – based on spatial considerations of light, views and privacy – to make the home suitable for the occupant. Facade cladding is also chosen from several options based on the dweller's preference and the coherence with the overall aesthetics of the surroundings.

With an innovative approach to solving living congestion and housing shortages in dense urban areas, Lighthouses are a possible solution for the forgotten areas of rooftops. They allow building owners and individuals alike to generate additional dwellings to meet today's rising demand for affordable housing.

Top left: Kitchen area.

Below left: Dining area.

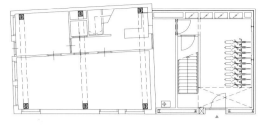

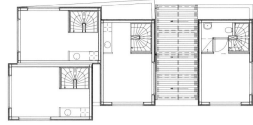

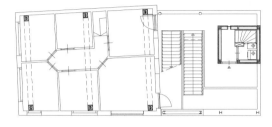

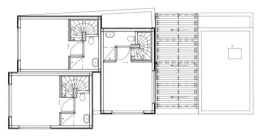

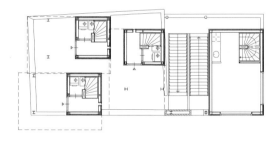

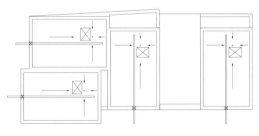

Top: Lower floor plan of the newly
installed modules.

Bottom: The upper floor of a newly
installed module.

Chapter 7
PREFABRICATED DWELLINGS

Digital and fabrication advances have renewed designers' interest in factory-built housing (Gonchar 2008). Contemporary prefabricated homes have shed the stigma that once saw them regarded as monotonous and technically inferior to conventionally constructed units (Trulove and Cha 2007). In Japan, for example, more than 120,000 houses per year – one third of all newly built homes – are made in a factory (Davies 2005). This rising trend can be attributed to their financial, environmental, structural and time-saving advantages (Elliot 2005, De Garrido 2008). Furthermore, constructing houses in a factory negates problems related to on-site construction such as vandalism, material storage and weather delays. Factories also require fewer skilled workers and therefore construction becomes cheaper. Another major advantage of prefabrication is the time consideration. An efficient, high-tech factory can produce a house in a week, in comparison to on-site construction, which, on average, takes more than five months (Elliot 2005).

There are three principal methods of prefabrication: modular, panellized and the kit-of-parts (Friedman 2005). Modular prefabrication consists of constructing large finished sections in the plant, which are then transported to a site, placed on a pre-prepared foundation and joined together with the help of a crane. This method requires the least site work. The panellized method involves manufacturing wall panels and floor sections, which are then shipped to a building site for assembly. In a kit-of-parts, a machine cuts each piece and labels it for site assembly by a skilled contractor. This method takes the longest to assemble and is more suitable for complex structures where saving time is less of a concern. There are numerous types of prefabricated systems, subsystems and components that can be combined at various levels to provide a complete system package. Panellized prefabrication, however, is probably the most widely used, therefore it is discussed below.

Nine types of panel systems are applicable to wood-frame residential construction. They can be divided into three categories: (1) open-sheathed panels (using conventional construction methods); (2) structural sandwich panels; and (3) unsheathed structural panels.

Open-sheathed panels (OSP): These are available in almost as many different variations as conventional wall construction. The most common systems are built with 38 x 140 mm (1.5 x 5.5 in) studs with plywood or waferboard sheathing, or with 38 x 89 mm (1.5 x 3.5 in) studs and extruded polystyrene sheathing. In either case, the panels are delivered open to the interior to facilitate the installation of electrical and/or plumbing services. Batt insulation is usually installed on-site, and is sometimes supplied by the manufacturer.

Structural sandwich panels (SSP): Also known as foam-core panels, these consist of a core of rigid foam insulation, which is laminated between two facing materials. In its most basic form, the sheathing materials may be either plywood or waferboard. More complete options offer exterior and/or interior finishes that replace the basic facing material and become an integral structural part of the panel.

The core material contains pre-cut electrical chases, and may be one of four different types of insulation: moulded bead expanded polystyrene; extruded polystyrene; polyurethane or polyisocyanurate. A variety of options are available for the joints between the panels.

Unsheathed structural panels (USP): USPs, or composite panels, are built using wood or metal structural elements combined with rigid foam insulation infill, usually expanded polystyrene. There are four basic variations of these systems available with different configurations for their structural elements, which provide a continuous thermal break and/or an air space in the interior of the panel. Horizontal chases for electrical wiring are often cut into the insulation to accommodate electrical wiring.

For each of the systems, it is possible to 'add value' to the panel by integrating a larger portion of the building envelope during fabrication. Added components vary from air barriers to exterior and/or interior finishes. The extent to which the panels are finished has different implications for the builder and the worker who will select and install the system.

One of the most significant advantages of prefabricated panel systems is the superior quality that can be achieved through the manufacturing process. This quality can be evaluated based on three interrelated characteristics: craftsmanship, technical performance and durability. The system's craftsmanship governs its potential to achieve consistent levels of performance from one application to another. The wall's technical performance, particularly with respect to its air-tightness, will affect the rate of deterioration due to condensation. Fire and sound resistance, critical for dividing walls, will contribute to the quality of the unit's interior environment. The panel's durability depends on the various materials' resistance to several elements, and on the probability of exposure to these, given the panels' designs.

Prefabricated panel systems are generally capable of technically outperforming walls built using conventional construction methods. Structural sandwich panel systems, particularly those with urethane or isocyanurate foam, provide excellent insulation value for a given thickness. This is partly due to their continuous

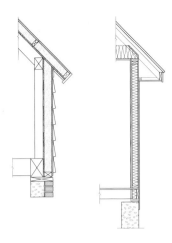

Figure 7.1 Comparison between panellized (left) and conventional (right) fabrication methods.

thermal break across the joints, particularly with the double spline variation. These panels also result in the tightest assemblies, due to their exceptionally well-fitted joint systems and the possibility of extending the exterior skin below the floor level, allowing for a continuous barrier across the end of the floor section. High performance levels are easy to achieve due to the inherent simplicity of the design. The critical nature of the lamination process, however, requires a relatively high level of quality control. Among the questionable characteristics of this panel type is a susceptibility of these systems to ridge at the joints because of inadequate allowance for thermal expansion, and the possibility of panels delaminating.

Unsheathed structural panels appear to provide good performance in all respects, but benefit from few extraordinary characteristics. The panels' biggest advantage is that they can overcome the inadequate workmanship that may be encountered in conventional construction without resorting to very unfamiliar building techniques. The use of expanded polystyrene foam between the structural elements significantly improves the performance of the wall in that area, which is a key failure point in conventionally built walls: discontinuous insulation and an air barrier caused by improper installation. Tight friction-fit joints and the ability to accommodate electrical boxes without interrupting the continuity of the insulation is an attractive advantage over conventional construction methods. Furthermore, the relatively simple manufacturing techniques (some make no use of adhesives) provide continuous thermal breaks and adequate air barriers, making them likely to achieve consistent performance levels.

As is the case with any manufactured component, the waste generated by the prefabrication of panel systems is less than could be expected from site construction. Assembly of the wall system in closed, controlled environments ensures that materials are used efficiently, and 'scrap' pieces of materials are more easily recovered and reused. Furthermore, the fact that the unit is closed within a short period of time reduces delays due to bad weather. Since there is less material wastage, the cost of clearing and removing debris is also lowered.

Despite the fact that prefabrication has already advanced as a result of innovation, there are plans to push the practice even further. These plans include using products made of recycled materials, online design and a choice of interior components by customers according to their spacial needs and budget (Duran 2008).

DRIVING FORCES

- Need to reduce cost
- Technological advances
- Need for energy efficiency
- Public interest in prefabrication

INNOVATIONS

- Better design and nicer appearance
- Automation/robotics
- Computer-aided design
- Multiple-use areas
- Higher energy efficiency standards

Figure 7.2 Wall sections of conventional wood-frame construction (left) and one with structural sandwich panels (right).

Figure 7.2

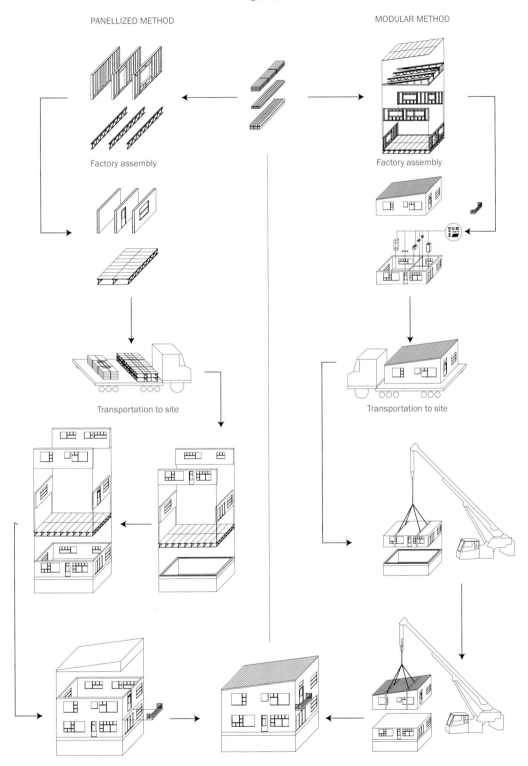

PANELLIZED METHOD

MODULAR METHOD

Factory assembly

Factory assembly

Transportation to site

Transportation to site

7.1 PREFABRICATED DWELLINGS

Project	Wood House in Caviano
Location	Caviano, Switzerland
Architect	Markus Wespi Jérôme de Meuron Architects BSA

Wood House is located in the hills at the edge of Caviano, Switzerland. The area, just outside the historical centre of Caviano, is filled with a mix of building types. Therefore, the intention of the architects Markus Wespi and Jérôme de Meuron, was to create a simple house that relates to the adjacent natural stonewalls rather than to the existing structures. The selection of inexpensive materials and the use of simple detailing optimized the overall cost of the 65-m^2

Top: The dark silver-grey tone of the facade blends in with the surrounding colours.

Right: Site plan.

Opposite page: Upper-floor living area (top), bedrooms floor (bottom)

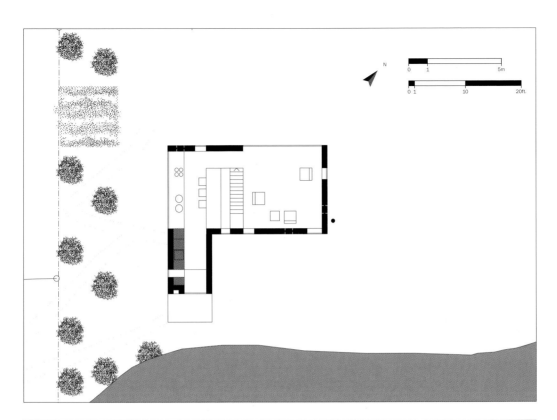

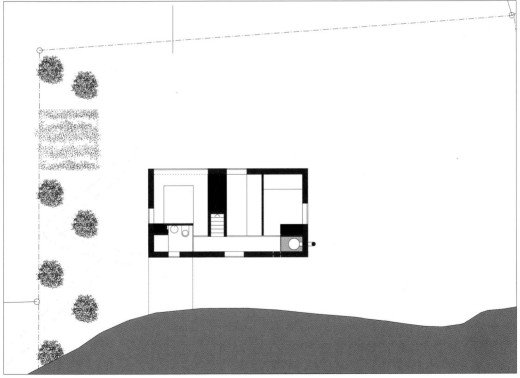

(700-sq ft) project. While the dark silver-grey toned facade blends in with the surrounding colours of the mountainous rocks, the use of prefabricated timber components both inside and outside is noticeable.

In general, without the use of drywall and baseboards to cover large areas, it is quite hard to produce modern detailing at a lower cost. Therefore, to enhance the visual experience without raising construction cost, the interior partitions, which were clad with oriented strand boards (OSB), remained exposed. Doors, cabinets and built-in tables were all made from OSB to achieve a uniform look. Similarly, they were painted in a dark silver-grey tone similar to that of the facade. In addition, no moulding or decorations were used where walls and glass partitions meet the floors and ceilings.

The two-level access provides direct entrances to both floors of the house. The kitchen and living areas are situated on the first floor in order to take advantage of the beautiful scenery. The ground floor contains three bedrooms and a washroom. To avoid unnecessary expenses and heat loss, the large, fixed windows differ from the smaller square ones, which can be opened for ventilation.

Below: Section showing the upper living area and the lower-level bedrooms.

Opposite page, top: West view.

Opposite page, bottom left: North view.

Opposite page, bottom centre: The kitchen area.

Opposite page, right: View from the living room.

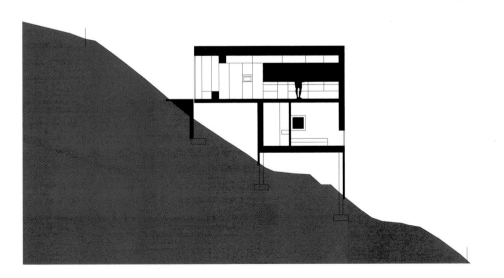

7.2 PREFABRICATED DWELLINGS

Project	Zufferey House
Location	Wallis (Valais), Switzerland
Architect	Nunatak Sarl

Located in Wallis, Switzerland, the Zufferey House is sited on a hilltop between the eastern and western L'Archavaz Mountains. Designed by Nunatak Architects Sarl, the dwelling's overall appearance, which can be interpreted both as complementing and contrasting to its environment, was inspired by the surrounding mountains and their visual qualities. The house has a total floor area of 185 m² (1,990 sq ft) on two levels. Nicknamed 'Angle', the house is aligned with the sloping elevation of the terrain and its facade is clad with natural grey slate that mimics the nearby rocks.

The house, which does not follow common vernacular construction practices, uses prefabricated panels, which save on labour and materials costs. Panellized wall sections were first

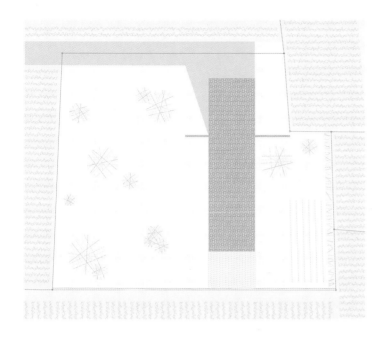

Left: Site plan.

Below: The shape of the house was inspired by the surrounding mountains.

manufactured and assembled in a factory, then shipped to the site for installation. The interior walls are covered by painted wood particle panels while the exterior panels contain thermal insulation. The house's grey, polished concrete flooring includes a heating system to form an 'active slab'. Indoors, there is a delightful combination of concrete slab and wooden ceilings and trims, as well as glass windows.

The living spaces, kitchen and guest bathrooms are located on the ground floor, and private bedrooms and bathrooms are on the first. The family's living space was extended to the outdoors by forming a terrace and a garden. Passive solar design principles also protect the occupants from summer heat and wind from the western valley. At the northern end of the house, the overhang design provides protection from the elements to the entrance and parking spaces.

Bottom left: View into the combined living, dining and kitchen areas.

Bottom right: The elongated stair and passageway along the exterior wall.

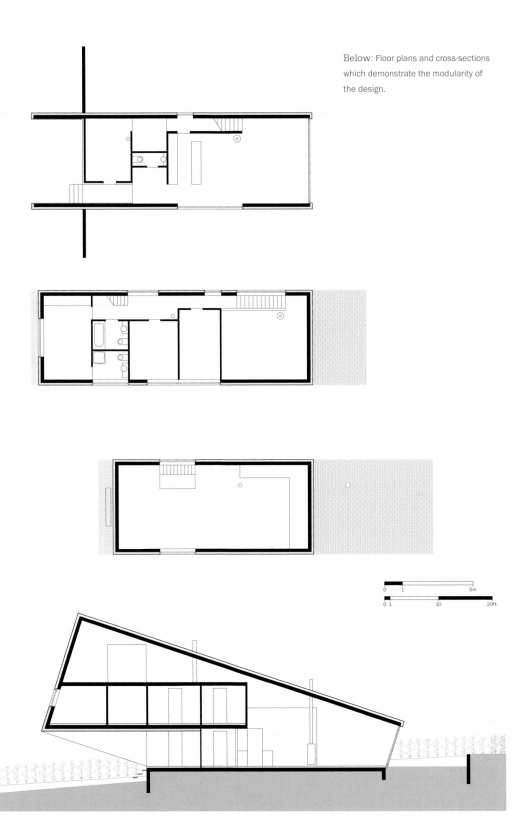

Below: Floor plans and cross-sections which demonstrate the modularity of the design.

0 1   5m
0 1   10   20ft.

Chapter 8
NARROW HOUSES

The design principles of narrow homes, which are often built in rows, date back to medieval times when property taxes were levied according to the width of the facade in dense walled cities. As a result, landowners sought to construct homes that were as narrow as possible. In North America, the design was common in many eastern cities until World War II when the desire to own a single-family, detached home led to a decline in the construction of narrow houses.

With the current realization that large homes are costly to maintain, builders, designers and consumers are once again exploring other housing prototypes. Furthermore, planners view low-density, detached dwellings as an unsustainable approach to land development. This perspective, coupled with the shrinking size of the family and rising energy costs, has led to renewed interest in narrow homes.

Although the definition of a narrow house is subjective, based on historical precedents, it can be suggested that it is a dwelling whose width measures up to 7.5 m (25 ft). Typically, it can be built as detached (stand-alone), semi-detached (two attached structures) or as part of a row or terrace. Detached, narrow houses are most commonly found in rural settings while semi-detached and terraced houses are frequently built in urban areas. Although each of these arrangements has its own unique characteristics due to their location and occupants, they share design aspects which maximize their efficiency and functionality while minimizing their environmental footprint.

One such characteristic has to do with their situation. Proper orientation will allow narrow dwellings to take advantage of passive solar heat gain. In rural areas, this means having one of the longer facades facing south or north, depending on latitude. Furthermore, this facade can contain large windows, for ease of solar exposure. In contrast, the opposite facade should have fewer openings and more insulation in order to minimize heat loss.

The relationship of these houses to each other is also significant when it comes to energy management. For example, a semi-detached structure with two narrow houses is 36 per cent more energy efficient than a detached house, while a unit in a terrace can be up to 64 per cent more efficient than a detached house (Friedman, 2005). This energy-use reduction can also be applied to air conditioning, which accounts for a large portion of the energy consumed.

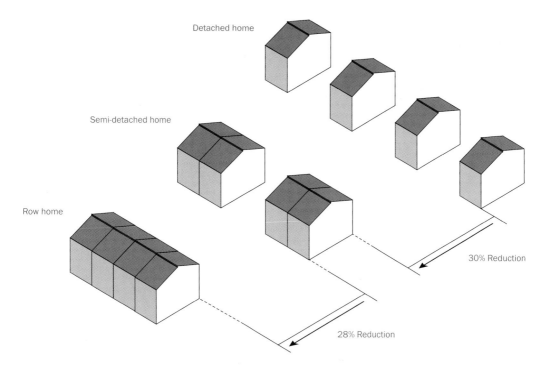

Detached home

Semi-detached home

Row home

30% Reduction

28% Reduction

The economic advantages of building houses in rows extend to other aspects as well. As population density increases, the cost of land and infrastructure decreases. Also, due to the small size of each unit, construction costs, material usage and waste are greatly reduced, which diminishes the house's environmental footprint. Additional environmental benefits of higher density planning include less need for residents to use cars, since very often the high density of households justifies the introduction of public transport and nearby commercial amenities, consequently cutting down greenhouse gas emissions.

A primary aspect that needs to be considered in narrow house design is interior spatial arrangement. One of the first things a designer does when working with narrow dwellings is to expand the perceived space. Careful placement of openings, for example, is a simple yet efficient method of achieving this. Large windows extend views beyond exterior walls and increase the amount of natural light. Balconies can be effective as well since they allow a physical and visual connection with the outside. They can be placed outside bedrooms or living rooms at the front or at the rear.

Another method used to expand the perception of space in narrow homes is to have an open-plan design. Traditional walls confine an area and limit exterior light penetration, making it feel smaller and darker. Partitions can be avoided by making rooms multifunctional. For example, a living room can also

Figure 8.1 Narrow homes built in a row are more energy efficient than detached units.

serve as a study, media or reading room, while the kitchen and dining room can be merged into one area. These rooms' spaces flow into each other and they share exterior views. When interior partitions are required, designers can use glass panels or blocks that prevent sound passage, but allow light to pass through (Oliver 2011). Installing sliding, translucent, Japanese-style screens is another way to divide or join spaces. Lastly, movable shelving units can be used as dividers since they can effectively enclose a space while also providing valuable storage.

Along with the spatial arrangement, designers of narrow homes must also consider the placement and organization of rooms and their various functions. It is a delicate process which, unlike with large dwellings, must be approached in a unique way. For example, the areas that are exposed to the greatest amount of light are generally located near the front and rear facades and, when a skylight exists, on the top floor. These spaces should be reserved for bedrooms and living rooms. As a result, the central spaces – which in a terraced house are darker – should be reserved for circulation and utilities.

Rooms that require more privacy are typically placed on upper floors. For example, in a two-level home, it is best to locate the bedrooms at the edges of the top floor and leave the core for circulation. The living room can be located at the rear of the ground/entrance level where it will receive more natural light and some privacy. The front of the ground floor should house the entrance and stairwell. The middle of the ground floor can be reserved for the kitchen and bathroom, which leaves the basement, if there is one, for storage and utilities. It is necessary to note that there are many other possible variations in a narrow dwelling's interior arrangement that would largely depend on

Figure 8.2 Optional stairs for narrow houses.

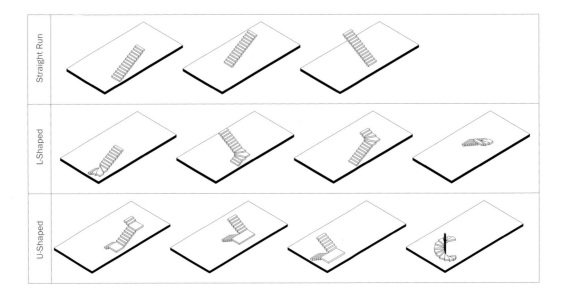

Straight Run	
L-Shaped	
U-Shaped	

cultural attitude, budget and the occupants' needs.

Due to its large effect on interior spatial arrangement, circulation should occupy as little space as possible. It is therefore important that the stairs be located close to the entrance, and that they proceed to the centre of the upper floor, which makes them accessible and avoids taking up valuable space. In general, there are four types of stairs suitable to narrow homes: circular, straight run, L-shaped and U-shaped. While the circular and straight-run stairs tend to be utilitarian in nature, the L-shaped and U-shaped stairs can form an atrium or a void. Such two-storey spaces can make the house seem much larger, since they allow more light to pass through. Designers have also resorted to creating open stairs with cantilevered steps and glass handrails that blend into the walls and, therefore, lessen their spatial impact.

Designers can also enhance the perceived size of the house by manipulating heights. A home with a taller ceiling feels larger without actually adding any area. Lower ceilings may create the opposite effect: intimate areas that can act in contrast to larger ones.

A well-designed narrow house can be space efficient, comfortable and affordable. The trend to reside in these homes may suggest that homebuyers are beginning to extend their thinking to consider the environmental effect that their chosen dwelling habits and lifestyles have.

DRIVING FORCES

- Economic downturn
- Smaller households
- High cost of land and infrastructure
- Higher energy costs

INNOVATIONS

- Invention of wide-span joists
- Adaptable design
- Wireless internal communication
- Demountable and moveable partitions

8.1 NARROW HOUSES

Project   Narrow House
Location   Tel Aviv, Israel
Architect   Ohad Yehieli

The Narrow House is located in a Tel Aviv neighbourhood that was originally developed in 1951 to house immigrants from Romania and Yemen. Although the district now houses commercial buildings and is slowly changing its character, the plot divisions still correspond to the original size of 63 m² (678 sq ft). At first glance, the dwelling's overall design is true to the modern, white-plastered walls of Tel Aviv's original Bauhaus style buildings. The challenge, however, was to design a house that measures only 3.7 m. (12 ft) wide, without openings on its 17 m. (56 ft) long sides. The house, designed by architect Ohad Yehieli for his family, offers functionality to suit contemporary lifestyles.

The house has a central staircase with a skylight that lets in light to the bathroom and the kitchen. The stairs also act as a ventilation shaft that allows air to flow from the ground floor to the upper levels. The occupants move through the core of the house to reach the relatively more open and illuminated ends of the home. Here, a more secluded space is created without side windows.

Above: The front view of the three storeys of Narrow House.

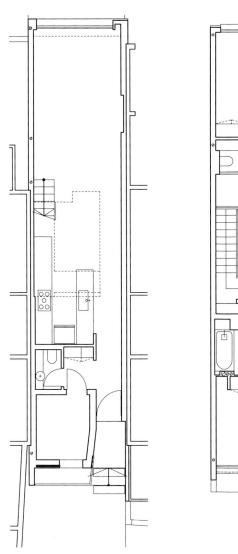

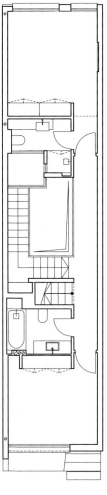

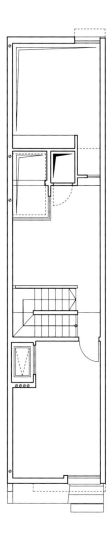

Above left: Ground floor with a
combined kitchen and living area.

Centre: The bedroom level.

Above right: Second floor.

At the two end facades, the reverse is applied. The openings are placed to balance between the proportions of windows and a view to the nearby park. Across the three floors, the family's living room and double-height bedroom at the rear are connected to the rear gardens and the surrounding views.

The neighbourhood is expected to see additional development and the construction of more narrow houses. For the time being, however, the white-plastered walls of the Narrow House set an inspiring example of both an authentic local tradition and a functional dwelling.

Above left: Long view of the entrance and passageway.

Above right: View of the two-storey-high living area.

Left: Site plan of the Narrow House with adjacent dwellings.

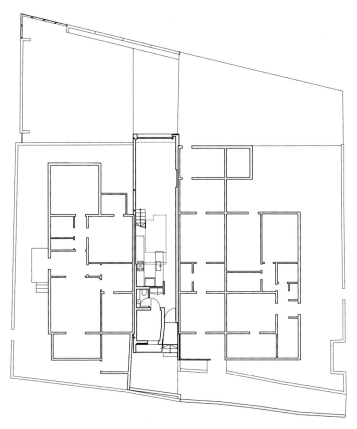

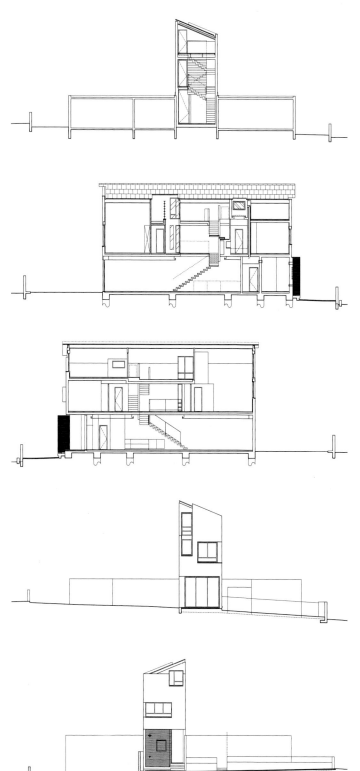

Left:

Top: Cross section

Below 1: Longitudinal section 1

Below 2: Longitudinal section 2

Below 3: Rear elevation

Bottom: Front elevation

8.2 NARROW HOUSES

Project   Layer House
Location   Kobe, Japan
Architect   Hiroaki Ohtani

In Japan, where the land is limited, space must be optimized. Urban dwellers must find creative ways to construct homes with a very small footprint. One of them is Hiroaki Ohtani. Both the owner and architect of Layer House, Ohtani has designed a unique and delightful narrow house between two existing row units in Kobe, Japan with a front facade that measures only 3.5 m (11.5 ft). Using pre-cast, stacked concrete strips to form a layering effect, the house was conceived as solid areas set against a void.

With no windows other than the front facade glass opening, it may seem to be tight and highly closed at first. However, with a split-level design that creates 76 m^2 (822 sq ft) of living area and combines the three floors, the Layer House seems cozy and has inviting qualities.

In the small and narrow dwelling, architect Ohtani paid close attention to circulation and spatial arrangement. The concrete slats create a progression throughout the length of the house, while avoiding spatial complexity and partitions that detracts from the unit's flow. Each structural layer is made up of cast concrete reinforced with pre-stressed steel rods. Through the roof and rear end, light enters the house after being divided into strips of illuminating rays. The stairs are cantilevered to reduce visual obstruction. In addition, wooden shelves, desks, clothing rods and

Above: The dwelling's walls are covered with intricate wooden lattice.

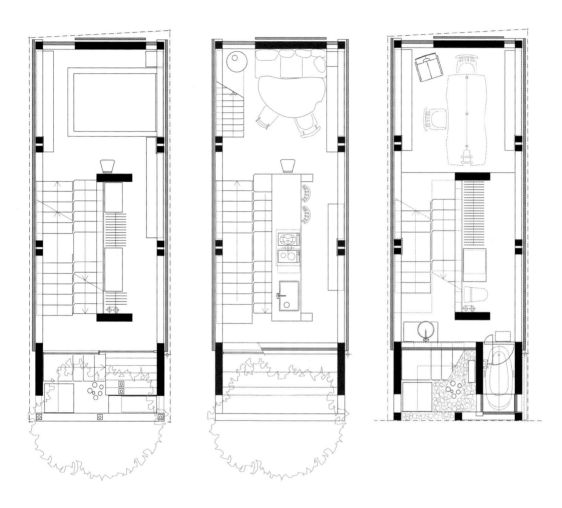

Above: The first floor shows the linearity of the unit.

Above centre: Second floor includes the kitchen and dining areas.

Above right: Basement level.

cabinets are also supported on the concrete slats, which helps make the house livable.

With a glass curtain wall that takes up the entire front facade, the floors are separated into lower, middle and upper levels that preserve the occupants' privacy. The kitchen and the living room are on the highest level, where they receive the most light. The bedroom is located at the rear end of the middle floor, which is slightly elevated from the street.

Given an exceptionally challenging task to create an infill unit in a very small area, Ohtani's design creatively separates the rooms on different levels while also managing to create a composition that pleasantly unites the house's individual elements.

Bottom left: Front elevation through which most of the natural light enters.

Bottom right: East-west section.

Opposite page, top left: A view into the open bedroom.

Opposite page, top right: An elongated view which demonstrates the narrowness of the dwelling.

Opposite page, bottom: The front curtain wall that lets in most of the natural light.

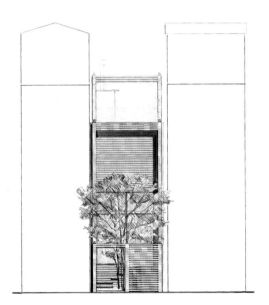

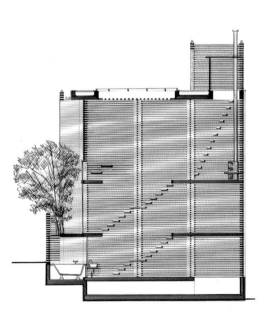

Chapter 9
PLUG AND PLAY DESIGNS

Plug and play homes are prefabricated, modular units that can be installed rapidly and ready for immediate use. In principle, with modern shipping techniques, plug and play dwellings can be transported to, or relocated, anywhere worldwide. Unlike prefabricated houses, which require some on-site assembly and are typically permanent, plug and play houses require no assembly and can be moved. The two main aspects affecting their conception are therefore transportation and interior design, which will be discussed below.

The design of plug and play units is determined by their need to be easily transported without causing external or internal damage. During transit, weight becomes a crucial factor, which permeates other design decisions. The goal is to create units that are heavy enough to sustain maximum wind drag when erected, but not too heavy as to exceed the supporting allowance on rooftops, for example (Studio Aisslinger 2011). For such rooftop units, the weight allowed varies greatly from unit to unit. Some firms claim that their units are rooftop safe with an average weight of 2,900 kg/m^2 (600 lb/sq ft), while others make the same claim with a weight of 230 kg/m^2 (47 lb/sq ft) to a max of 820 kg/m^2 (170 lb/sq ft) (Alchemy Architects 2011, Studio Aisslinger 2011). Regardless of the varying weights, however, it is important to verify roofing allowances before placing a plug and play home atop a flat roof.

Designing to facilitate transportation also involves protecting external building components. Windows and doors present a special challenge since they weaken the overall structure and are breakable. Rather than compromising and limiting the numbers of windows and doors, however, designers have developed methods to protect them during travel. One method consists of large, sliding protective panels over the windows. This allows for the design of units in which the facades are almost entirely made of glass. Furthermore, some designers have created units in which the doors and windows fold into the structure to protect them, which also provides more interior space when installed. It is also possible to use thick shutters, which can be closed to seal off the glass and add structural support, much like on hurricane-proof buildings. Designers have also suggested units that can mechanically retract inwards to protect them during transportation, and can then be extended back out at the push of a button (Galvagni 2011).

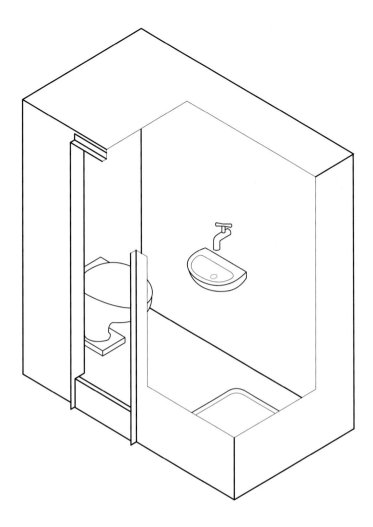

Protection of the interior is another factor that must be considered in plug and play homes, since furniture and appliances can be damaged during transportation. One of the best ways to solve this is by bolting down all appliances and having furniture built into the walls and floors (Aisslinger 2009).

Since plug and play houses are generally small, designers must consider interior design for a limited space. The goal is to create spaces that feel large while still being efficient and functional. While this includes many of the concepts covered in the chapter on small dwellings (see page 42), there are a number of principles that are uniquely relevant to plug and play homes. Furthermore, there exists an assumption that modular, transportable units are cheap and uncomfortable, and while this may have been true in the past, recent innovation and technology has created high-tech, aesthetically pleasing structures, which are sleek, efficient and light (Nio and Kuenzli 2003). In fact, because plug and play homes are smaller and

Figure 9.1 A prefabricated bathroom designed for use in a Plug and Play home.

less costly than traditional dwellings, designers are able to use more expensive materials, sophisticated technologies and customizable features to make them affordable and comfortable (Solomon 2011, Assasi 2008).

Where internal separation is needed it is possible to use sliding panels, which allow the occupant to customize the space (Studio Aisslinger 2011). Although these panels can range from translucent to opaque, it is recommended that they allow as much light through them as possible. Also, by placing the entrance stairs along the exterior wall, more space can be used for living. These stairs can also be designed to fold up or detach during transportation. Although the stairs can be made from any materials, it is recommended that a lightweight material, such as aluminium, be used due to its strength (Aisslinger 2009).

Built-ins are one method used to increase space efficiency; they are a useful tool to use when re-designating interior areas throughout the day, since beds, benches and tables can often be hidden in the walls and folded out when needed. It is also possible to create multi-use built-ins. In the LoftCube by Studio Aisslinger, for example, the shower head can easily be swivelled to serve as a watering hose for interior vegetation (Studio Aisslinger 2011).

The idea of built-ins can also be extended to the arrangement of utilities. To save space and minimize clutter, some designers have taken to embedding heating and cooling in the floors and walls. Furthermore, the dwellings are typically designed so that the windows, or roof, can open up to let outdoor air circulate within, which acts as natural air-conditioning. Many units are also equipped with mechanical ventilation systems (Aisslinger 2009).

Although plug and play homes require attachment of basic utilities, it is likely that future models will be off-grid designs. With improvements in technology such as solar cell development, battery life, water purification/recycling facilities and sewage cleaning facilities, it is plausible that some modules in future will be completely self-sufficient.

Many plug and play homes contain materials such as LED-lit frosted glass panels, marble countertops, floor-to-ceiling windows and lush carpets. In fact, they are constructed as 'smart houses', in which appliances and lighting are digitally controlled by a single touch-screen pad (Assasi 2008, Studio Aisslinger 2011).

Furthermore, these units can sometimes be designed with customizable features, such as shutters and interior walls. In the Loftcube design for example, the selection of shutters and windows is easily customized to allow each unit to have different levels of privacy. The shutter systems can be independent for windows or facades, thereby permitting greater privacy control.

It is also possible to customize the units for future expansion by leaving room for the attachment of other modules. The function of these attachments can vary from home offices to new bedrooms, according to the needs of the inhabitant. While this is one way to solve issues related to live–work, expandable, adaptable and multigenerational dwellings, designers have also developed ideas for the assembly of a number of units. These assembled units are designed to be plugged into larger networks called 'megastructures'. Some of the designs form housing towers, while others are ground level (Assasi 2008). In fact, to a large extent, some projects of this type already exist: both Habitat 67 in Montreal, Canada and the Nakagin Capsule Tower in Tokyo, Japan were made of modular units. Contrary to the plug and play ideals however, modules from both these megastructures are very difficult, if not impossible to relocate (Assasi 2008).

Plug and play homes also have other applications. Firms, such as Lab Zero, are choosing to refurbish used shipping containers to promote the idea of re-use and recycling (Galvagni 2011). Some of these attempts are quite successful and have created cutting-edge architecture. Other firms are targeting prefabrication of affordable housing to be delivered to customers around the world, similar to the automobile industry, for example.

DRIVING FORCES

- Need to shorten construction times
- Built structures for a short duration and use
- Advances in prefabrication
- Need for urban densification

INNOVATIONS

- Advances in shipping techniques
- Development of lightweight materials
- Development of modular bathroom and kitchen units
- Innovation in small space design
- Refurbish shipping containers

9.1 PLUG AND PLAY DESIGNS

Project   Loftcube

Location   New York, New York, USA

Architect   Studio Aisslinger

High house prices have made home ownership difficult in many cities. Urban hubs like New York and London can only attract individuals for temporary stays, job opportunities or study.

The German architect Werner Aisslinger's project, Loftcube, offers a dwelling that suits people with a 'nomadic' lifestyle and allows for temporary stays in dense urban areas. While its economic incentive is to market unused real estate in urban locations, the Loftcube is in fact a transportable penthouse that can be placed on rooftops, or other terrain such as mountaintops, islands and in forests.

The cube measures 55 m^2 (588 sq ft) and is made of a steel and wood frame. To meet the demands of temporary living, the cube's weight is calculated to allow transportation by helicopter and positioning by crane, while being structurally sturdy and heavy enough to withstand wind forces. For oversees transportation, the kit can be stored in a 12 m (40 ft) long container, and can be transported by cargo ship. Installation time from the initial placement of the cube to full living

Below: A view of a Loftcube unit.

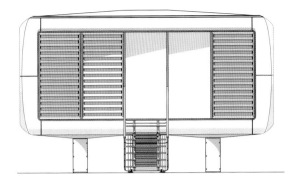

This page: The four facades of the
Loftcube. The lightness of the unit was
achieved by using glass curtain walls.

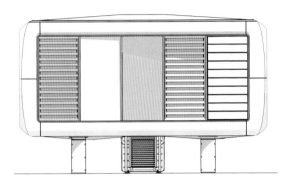

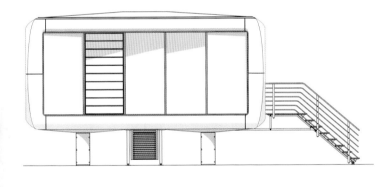

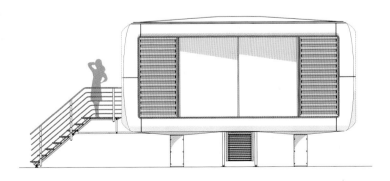

access for occupants can take as little as two days. Furthermore, many urban buildings are able to accommodate the additional weight of the Loftcube and no labour-intensive work is needed for their installation.

The envelope can be clad with a wide selection of materials. Ranging from transparent glass panels for views of the outdoors to opaque timber louvres that help retain privacy. Buyers can choose whatever is most suitable to their lifestyle and location.

Indoors, the pod provides a 360-degree panoramic view. Even though there are four general spaces (living, kitchen, bathroom and bedroom), partitioning is installed for multifunctional usage. For example, both the kitchen and bathroom sinks share a common manoeuvrable tap. Portable furniture and sliding tracks can be constantly adjusted, so as to not to obscure the indoor view and light.

Below: The interior of the Loftcube was designed efficiently and includes all basic functions.

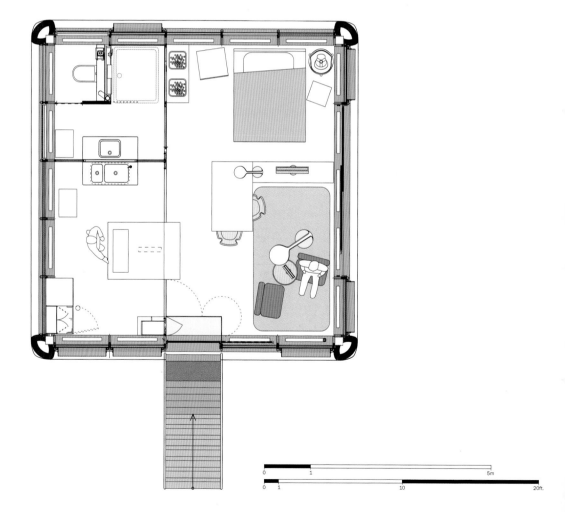

Above: Lifting the Loftcube onto a rooftop.

Left: Transporting the Loftcube.

Bottom Left: Open plan and glass curtain walls helped alleviate the effect of a small-sized unit.

9.2 PLUG AND PLAY DESIGNS

Project	Arado weeHouse
Location	Ontario, Canada
Architect	Alchemy Architects

As a weekend cabin, studio, family home or an addition to an existing dwelling, the weeHouse, designed by Alchemy Architects in Ontario, Canada, is a dwelling that can accommodate a wide range of living demands and locations. Fabricated from a steel and wood frame in a factory, the unit can be delivered to any site by truck.

On-site, an installation crew takes approximately four to eight hours to bolt the unit to a foundation, which can be piers or perimeter. For occupants who wish to expand, there is room for the addition of more storage and a full basement. For dwellers who plan to live in the unit for a short period of time, piers are a more suitable foundation for labour and materials savings in case of dismantling. In partnership with independent plants in the USA and Canada, Alchemy works to economize time, budget and transportation.

It takes about six to nine weeks to prefabricate the frame and install tongue-and-groove bamboo flooring, interior gypsum board walls and furnishings. The standard weeHouse area is 41 m² (438 sq ft) and it is clad with corrugated steel, available in a range of colours and finishes to be selected by the dweller. Depending on the occupant's request, appliances, cabinets and fixtures can also be added to the basic unit. In an effort to complement locations with extreme weather, Alchemy can choose to install in-floor heating and small air-conditioning units

Above: The weeHouse can be installed in four to eight hours.

Opposite top: The two glass facades let in light that makes a small space seem big.

Opposite below: A view into the space-efficient kitchen and dining areas.

that can be hidden in a back cabinet. On the other hand, clients who wish to purchase just a weeHouse 'shell' and finish it themselves can do so. The unit can also be custom-designed for the particular needs of each dweller.

Other factory-produced modules by the same designers include larger weeHouses, with stairs to an upper level, full-sized kitchen, garage and sleeping spaces. They are affordable in comparison to conventionally built houses and can be easily adapted to various sites.

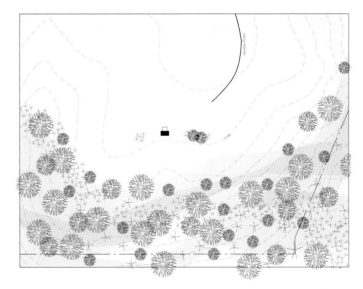

Top: Floor plan of the weeHouse.

Middle: Longitudinal section.

Middle: Cross section 1.

Bottom: Cross section 2.

Opposite, top: The weeHouse can be placed on several types of foundation, among them concrete pile, shown here.

Opposite, bottom: The siting of the unit minimizes damage to nature.

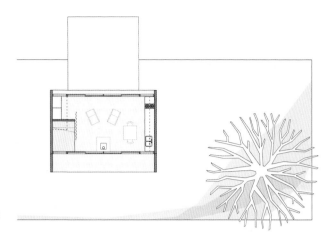

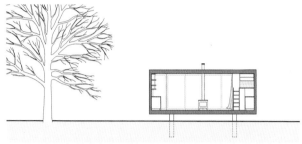

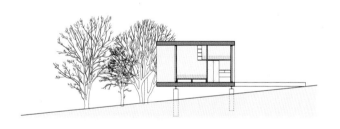

Chapter 10
HEALTHY INDOOR ENVIRONMENTS

The design thrust of a home with a healthy indoor environment is to ensure the occupants' health and comfort. Aspects such as lighting, ventilation, temperature control and pollutants, among others, are considered in order to prevent conditions that can occur in poorly designed spaces. This can be a challenging task since the standards of comfort are subjective. Despite these variations, there are four key factors that are vital to the design of a space in most situations: thermal comfort, visual comfort, indoor air quality (IAQ)/ventilation and materials selection, each of which will be elaborated on below.

At the outset, a healthy indoor environment must be thermally comfortable. A properly designed thermal system keeps a balance between body heat loss and gain so that a person can maintain homeostasis without effort (Encyclopaedia Britannica 2011a). Due to the subjective nature of what a comfortable temperature is, it is difficult to create conditions that suit every occupant. Therefore, one of the more effective ways to design a thermal system is to control variables that influence indoor temperature and give as much control as possible to the inhabitant. Designers need to consider indoor air temperature, relative humidity, surface or radiant temperature and air speed.

Visual comfort is another important topic in the design of healthy indoor environments, since a lack of consideration can lead to several health problems. Poor lighting for example, can lead to eye strain, headaches, fatigue and lack of concentration. Therefore, it is important to properly consider the visual requirements of each space and design it accordingly. To do this, the design should take into consideration type and quality of light, openings and their control.

Air quality and ventilation is a major consideration. Because people spend 80 to 90 per cent of their time indoors, any polluted or under-circulated air can quickly lead to problems such as allergies, mould, asthma and the transfer of infectious diseases (Craig et al. 2004). To avoid such problems – or what is otherwise known as 'sick building syndrome' – it is important to create an airtight building, which prevents unintentional air leakage and achieves maximum control over the airflow (Bas 2004). Furthermore, this extends to other principles, such as expelling pollutants through ventilation, properly filtering indoor air and identifying and removing sources of pollution.

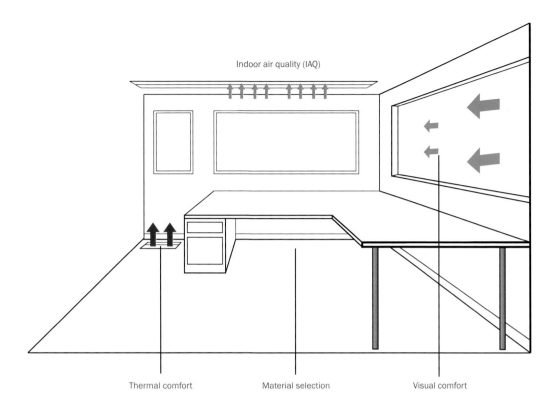

Indoor air quality (IAQ)

Thermal comfort   Material selection   Visual comfort

Finally, building materials and their selection are very important in creating healthy indoor environments. While some materials are harmless, others, from furnishings or certain adhesives used in construction, can give off toxic gases. Sometimes, these toxic fumes are only released for a short period, but in other cases the emission process can last for years. Unfortunately, both natural and man-made materials can be either safe or toxic. Therefore, it is important to select materials based on how their qualities will affect the occupants. Special attention should be given to future maintenance requirements, emission test reports and the production process of the materials.

When the details of a home with a healthy indoor environment are discussed, one needs to recognize that a dwelling's thermal comfort is reliant upon its air temperature; this is best controlled by a thermostat that can be adjusted to suit the occupants' needs. Relative humidity is another factor that affects thermal comfort by influencing body heat loss. Differing levels of moisture in the air can affect moisture evaporation resulting in the increase or decrease of the perceptual temperature (Kwok and Grondzik 2007). Therefore, it is recommended that the relative humidity be kept at acceptable levels, which range between 30 per cent and 60 per cent, depending upon the season (Bas 2004).

Figure 10.1 The four key factors affecting the indoor environment are noted above.

Surface, or radiant, temperature is also an important consideration. In winter, poor thermal insulation may create cold internal surfaces, necessitating excessively warm air. In summer however, surfaces gain heat through exposure to direct sunlight. Hot surfaces in the house create unwanted increases of indoor air through convection (Encyclopaedia Britannica 2011b). It is therefore necessary to integrate shading devices or take advantage of nearby trees for shading.

Visual comfort is typically based on the type of light that reaches each space. Of the two types of light, daylight and artificial light, daylight is recommended because it is soft, diffused, creates little glare and does not increase the radiant temperature. Despite the advantages of daylight, it is also important to have adequate artificial lighting in each space for nightfall. This artificial light should mimic daylight as closely as possible and should be placed in such a way that it gets maximum distribution. Subsequently, appropriate openings need to be included to increase the amount of natural daylight. This will also improve the internal space's quality by perceptually extending its size and characteristics into the exterior. Lastly, it is important to control lighting to avoid otherwise unwanted glare or night-time outdoor lights. These can greatly decrease the visual comfort of a dwelling. Tools such as movable shutters, adjustable light fixtures, skylights, high-efficiency lighting, well-illuminated work areas and trees for natural shade are all important in the control of natural and artificial light

Indoor air quality (IAQ) and ventilation are chiefly controlled through the expulsion of pollutants through appropriate ventilation systems. These systems need to be evenly distributed to prevent drafts, varying temperatures between spaces, low circulation areas where pollutants can be gathered and high

Figure 10.2 Measures that can be taken to reduce heat loss by sealing the envelope of a wood-frame building.

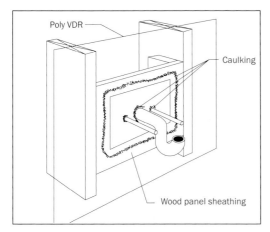

Sealing the envelope after plumbing penetration

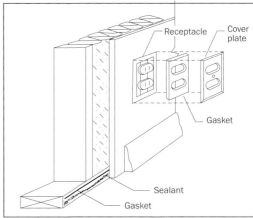

Sealing the envelope at an electrical outlet

moisture areas where bacteria and mould can grow. Placing the supply ports far away from the return vents can do this, allowing air to be properly circulated throughout a space before being drawn back into the exhaust vents. Ample air intake into a properly maintained heating, ventilation and air conditioning (HVAC) system – or a system with baseboard heaters and a heat recovery ventilator (HRV) – is also important to ensure that all used air is replaced. Furthermore, since the ventilation systems are often places where pollutants and mould build up, their inherent filtration systems should be regularly cleaned to avoid spreading such problems throughout the house. Special filters to remove gaseous pollutants, such as activated charcoal filters or other absorbent products, are available if needed (Aller Air Purifiers 2009). Lastly, IAQ can be improved by identifying and removing sources of pollution. One way to do this is to ensure that external supply vents are taking in clean outdoor air by placing intake vents away from polluted outdoor sources such as neighbouring exhaust vents.

While quantifying material pollutant emissions is a new science with many unknown implications, there are still some important general aspects to note. One of them is that neither natural nor fabricated products emit fewer pollutants: each product is unique. For example, chipboard may appear to be environmentally friendly because it is fabricated from woodchips; however, it also uses toxic binders (Public Works and Government Services Canada 2009). Furthermore many natural products degrade faster and therefore may require toxin emitting treatments. Other natural products such as arsenic, formaldehyde and asbestos are inherently toxic and considered dangerous. Therefore, it is necessary to look at emission test reports, which can be found with common materials like carpets and engineered wood products. If an emission test report cannot be found, then the product in question should be chosen with caution, or avoided entirely.

Designers should also be aware that materials that are initially safe might require an application of toxic preservatives in future to extend their life and that such implications should be considered during the initial design phase. Despite the danger of toxic materials, it can be difficult to detect which materials might be harmful since there are some cases where testing is not common or standardized. In these cases, one should look for common factors that might indicate the presence of toxins products, such as adhesives, vinyl, polymerization and foam expansion.

DRIVING FORCES

- Increased public interest in indoor air quality
- Use of harmful compounds in construction
- Improved mechanical ventilation systems
- Less reliance on mechanical ventilation vs. fresh air technologies

INNOVATIONS

- Improvement in building science and construction
- New ventilation and heat recovery technologies
- New artificial lighting technologies
- Development of non-emitting bonding materials

10.1 HEALTHY INDOOR ENVIRONMENTS

Project   NEXTHouse
Location   Seattle, Washington, USA
Architect   David Vandervort Architects

The Magnolia neighbourhood in Seattle, Washington is located on hilly terrain in the American Northwest, enclosed by the waters of Elliot Bay and surrounded by views of the Cascade Mountains. This landscape, mixed with the Pacific coastal climate, gave opportunities for the firm David Vandervort Architects to design a healthy and comfortable dwelling. The project NEXTHouse was constructed on a plot after an existing home was demolished due to its inability to meet the occupants' needs. The new house, measuring 228 m² (2,750 sq ft), was designed with principles of healthy living in mind, both for the dwellers and the environment at large.

The NEXTHouse is orientated east–west to take full advantage of the southern sun exposure. While the region is known for a large amount of precipitation and

Below: The NEXTHouse is oriented east-west to take full advantage of the southern sun exposure.

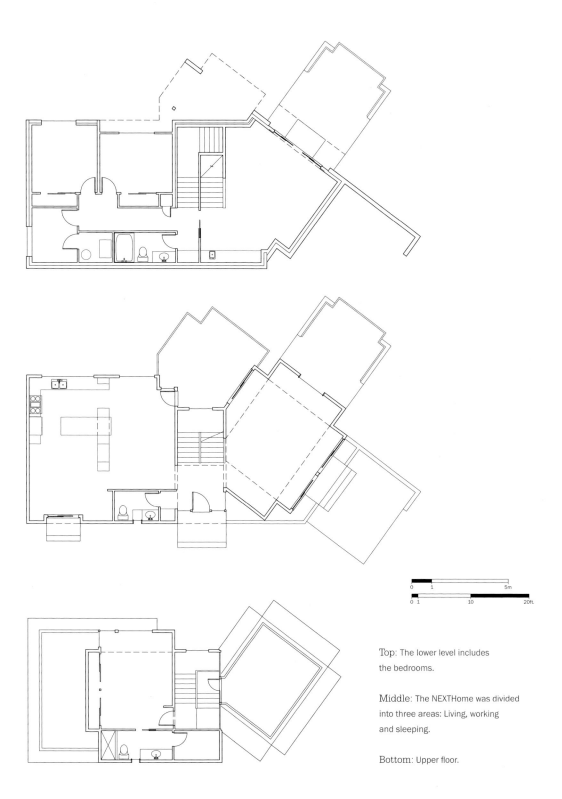

Top: The lower level includes
the bedrooms.

Middle: The NEXTHome was divided
into three areas: Living, working
and sleeping.

Bottom: Upper floor.

clouds, window openings have been placed all around the three-storey house to provide adequate natural light and to minimize the use of artificial illumination. The combination of the centrally located stairwell and the clerestory windows on the higher level triggers a 'stack effect' to create an upper draft between the floors to further cool down the dwelling in the summer.

The design consists of three main zones: living, working and sleeping. Each space has openings that lead to patios and decks to provide access to the outdoors. Overhanging roofs act as a shading device that prevents overexposure to sunlight, which could cause an uncomfortable glare. By using

components with low volatile organic compound (VOC) paint finishes and formaldehyde-free plywood, all the materials that were used in the interior are non-toxic and provide a healthy indoor environment. It is also worth noting that the NEXTHouse was constructed using materials that were recycled from the house that previously stood on the site.

To ensure a comfortable indoor temperature in the changing seasons, walls are insulated with sprayed polyurethane foam, while a hydronic radiant heating system was installed in the floors. Furthermore, the green roof contains vegetation that helps lower heating needs and offers additional insulation. In the winter months, when the windows

are closed, a heat exchange ventilation system assists in the circulation to further improve airflow and foster healthy indoor air. The roof also integrates a 1-kW, thin film of solar array and includes a metering system that allows the occupants to be aware of their energy generation and consumption.

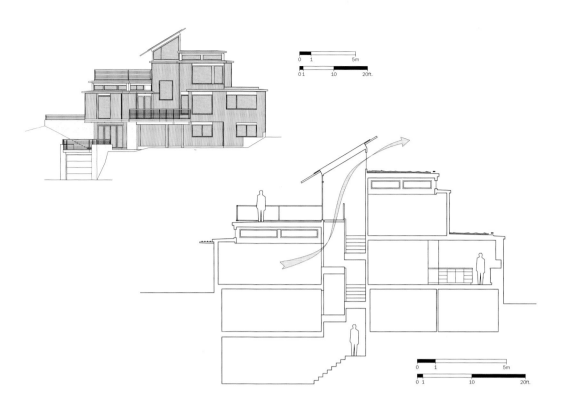

Top: The facade of the NEXTHouse.

Middle: The stairwell and the clerestory triggers a stack effect and a draught between the floors.

Left: View of the rear porch.

Opposite, far left: The house was constructed with materials that were recovered from an old dwelling that stood on the same site.

Opposite, left: No materials with Volatile Organic Compounds (VOCs) were used in construction.

10.2 HEALTHY INDOOR ENVIRONMENTS

Project | Steel Study House II
Location | Leeuwarden, The Netherlands
Architect | Archipelontwerpers

Built on the perimeter of Leeuwarden, in the north of Holland, Steel Study House II is situated in a transitional space between an urban area and agricultural land. For this reason, it defies the typical morphology of its locale and is built surrounding an open-air patio, which operates as a central hub, as a way of embodying that transition. The layout intersperses enclosed areas with wide open spaces connected to the outside, and many spaces are only partly bound by walls.

The facades of Steel Study House II differ based on their position in relation to the urban and open areas. The western facade, which faces the town, is designed to integrate with surrounding buildings. A ramp allows entrance from the pavement and public urban areas, but motorized blinds have been installed to allow the inhabitants to visually cut off the built environment should they choose. The opposite facade, on the other hand, includes breathtaking views of wide-open, uninhabited spaces and the adjacent lake.

All of the rooms in the house also have a view of the interior patio, further breaking the separation between room and open space. As a result, each room has at least some direct connection to the open air. This gives the inhabitants a sense of always being part of a larger open space. Passage from room to room will often take the occupant through one or more open area, thus ensuring that the air is always fresh.

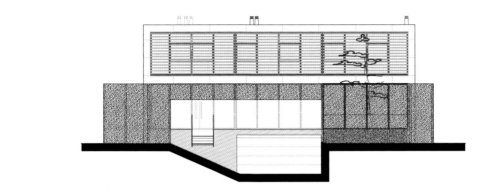

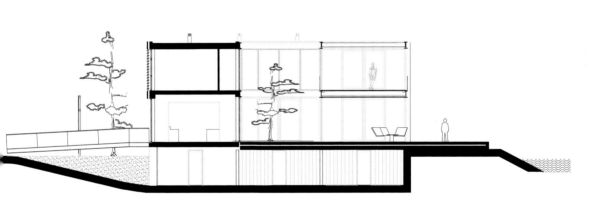

Opposite page, top: The rear elevation
faces the water.

Opposite page, bottom: The house is
situated in a transitional space between
urban and agricultural areas.

Top: East elevation

Above: A section showing the
entrance ramp.

Left: A view of the patio that faces the water.

Opposite, top: All the rooms in the house have views of the interior patio.

Opposite, bottom: The open plan design lets air circulate.

In a society that is becoming increasingly aware of its toll on the environment, common housing design and construction practices are being re-examined in order to lessen their environmental impact. The proliferation of the large detached home and its many negative consequences, primarily in North America, supports evidence that local actions have a global effect. It has also become evident that changes to these practices are urgently needed if the effects of these actions are to be reversed.

At the core of those changes lies the recognition that the world's natural resources are being depleted faster than the Earth is able to renew them. Lumber, iron ore and fossil fuels, for example, are among those materials whose stock is rapidly disappearing.

The need to develop housing prototypes that consume fewer resources and recycle others during their fabrication and occupancy is an urgent priority. Homes that generate their own power or use very little, take advantage of the sun for energy generation, use construction products made from recycled material and are water efficient are some of the concepts that will be discussed here.

Chapter 11
NET-ZERO DWELLINGS

Net-zero dwellings reduce energy consumption and hold the potential to find equilibrium in power usage and generation by decreasing reliance on the electric grid. These houses divert the generation of power away from polluting, conventional power plants and into local, more sustainable and cleaner methods. Although there are many definitions of a net-zero home, it can be defined as a house that produces and returns as much energy to the grid as it uses.

An important factor to consider when designing a net-zero building is the method used to heat and cool the structure. Since typical mechanical systems account for around 55 per cent of the overall energy consumption, net-zero housing can only be successful if its heating and cooling systems take advantage of natural sources (Baumann 2009). Factors such as insulation, waste-water heat recovery, window type and quality, natural ventilation, building envelope, green roofs and thermal storage areas contribute to the performance of a dwelling as much as, if not more, than the heating and air-conditioning systems themselves.

Another principle of net-zero dwellings is their energy production method. For a house to qualify for net-zero status,

Figure 11.1: The three principles of Net-Zero building are: energy efficiency, power generation and the feeding of power back to the grid.

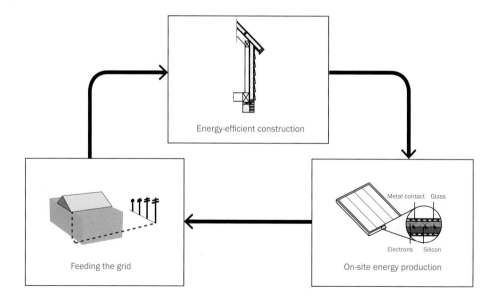

Energy-efficient construction

Feeding the grid

On-site energy production

Metal contact   Glass

Electrons   Silicon

it must produce as much energy as it uses. It is important to decide whether the dwelling will be off-grid – using batteries to store energy for low production times – or grid-tied – in which case the dwelling can draw from and give back to the local power grid. This decision will affect the type of system chosen and therefore the cost, but whether the homes are off-grid or grid-tied, to qualify as net-zero they cannot emit any carbon dioxide (Tanha 2010). Although this immediately rules out the use of fossil fuel furnaces, there are still many applicable systems, such as photovoltaic panels and wind turbines, to choose from. Furthermore, it is best to combine these electricity production methods with other heat-production methods such as geothermal pumps and solar hot water vacuum tubes. While such heat-production systems do not actually produce electricity, they are valuable in reducing the amount required to heat the dwelling, making electrical production more effective.

Another principle of net-zero dwellings that decreases their energy consumption is their size and orientation. Aspects such as the building's dimensions and site orientation are critical to taking effective advantage of passive solar gain, natural daylight and indoor airflow. There are also much larger decisions that both designers and clients must consider before even purchasing a site, such as the local wind patterns, sun orientation, topography, the ground depth of winter frost and shadows cast by other buildings and trees.

Finally, there are many digital devices that can help both the construction of net-zero dwellings, and their maintenance. Such technologies range from sun, wind and heat capacity calculating software to smart thermostats and energy usage readers.

Figure 11.2: Alternative means of energy production in a net-zero building.

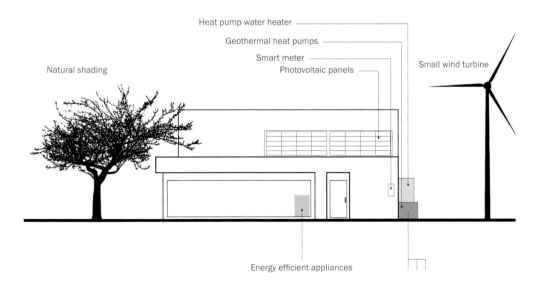

Heat pump water heater

Geothermal heat pumps

Smart meter

Photovoltaic panels

Small wind turbine

Natural shading

Energy efficient appliances

A net-zero house must be well insulated to reduce air leakage through the walls, floors and ceiling. There are several ways to do this. More traditional methods include the mixing of commonly used insulators such as the combination of open-cell spray foam and cellulose insulation in the wall, floors and roof with rigid insulation on the exterior (Macht 2010). Some designers though, opt for innovative techniques such as thick-wall, wrap-and-strap, double-wall and truss-wall. It is also possible to use cutting-edge thermal barrier materials; however, due to the increased expense of such innovative methods they should be reviewed to verify their cost-effectiveness before use (Tanha 2010). Regardless of whether a traditional mix or innovative approach is chosen, it is important that every net-zero dwelling is carefully sealed with a membrane to prevent air flowing through the walls. Since this is already commonplace among most current housing standards, it is relatively easy to obtain the appropriate specifications and guidelines.

When using a tightly insulated membrane, it is important to maintain airflow throughout the structure using suitable heating ventilation and air-conditioning (HVAC) methods or heat-recovery ventilation (HRV). These appliances recover the heat as it flows outside and transfer it into the new, fresh air that is entering the building. This is a very efficient method to reduce wasted energy though heat loss. Waste-water recovery systems perform the same functions for water and transfer heat from used water into potable water before it flows into the sewage system (Macht 2010).

The proper selection of windows and doors is another key factor in the energy management of a net-zero dwelling since they are critical to preventing unwanted heat loss or gain. One of the more widely used types of glass in net-zero buildings is krypton gas-filled low-emissivity glass, which is available in double- or triple-pane windows and doors. With such high thermal performance, these windows can be up to four times more efficient than traditional double-pane windows, but can have a large price tag (Macht 2010). Their usage should therefore be planned carefully for maximum efficiency. Another, more innovative, glass type is electrochromic or thermochromic glass. It contains glazing which can change from opaque to transparent instantly, and helps to control sunlight penetration and glare (Gonchar 2010).

Natural ventilation is another way to use natural cycles of hot and cold air to create airflow in a dwelling, and therefore reduce the use of air conditioning during summer months. This operates on the principle that hot air is less dense than cold air and therefore rises while cold air sinks. Designing a house to have windows near the ground and others near the top of a room is vital to taking advantage of this cycle (Tanha 2010). It is also important to design a structure with high ceilings, which encourages airflow throughout the dwelling (Haran 2009).

This air cycle can also be extended to the building envelope. Since the 'skin' is exposed to more solar energy than any other part of the building, it can be a great asset to gaining free energy. Current innovative techniques for such purposes include those that allow cold, sinking air to enter and be trapped in a thin layer between a steel mesh and the building wall. Here, the air is subjected to heat from the sun and, as it heats up and rises, it is collected and pumped either into the house or into thermal storage areas from which it is drawn and used to regulate the temperature (Gonchar 2010).

Designers of net-zero housing use two types of thermal reservoirs: green roofs and basement crawlspaces. Both methods rely on absorbing heat during the day, thereby keeping the house cooler, and releasing that heat at night to keep the dwelling warmer (City of Vancouver 2010). It is important to note that when a basement or crawlspace exists, heat storage only works on the first 10 cm (4 in) of any wall (Tanha 2010, Gonchar 2010).

The production of energy is also key to the design of net-zero homes, and the location of the building may very well prove to be the deciding factor on the form that energy production takes. When producing electricity with wind power, it is important to keep in mind that air density and average wind speed in an area can determine which turbine will be most effective (Tanha 2010). With solar power, it is important to review sun-path diagrams to determine the best location and angle at which to place photovoltaic cells for maximum solar intensity and duration. For solar hot water production there are several models which should be reviewed, such as the flat-plate, the evacuated tube and the integral collector (Tanha 2010, City of Vancouver 2010).

One of the most effective ways to improve the performance of a net-zero home is through its orientation and footprint size. To benefit most from passive solar gain, the house should be orientated towards the sun and have overhanging shades on the windows that respect the sun angles as determined by sun-path charts.

New computing techniques are advantageous in net-zero dwellings for both the designer and homeowner. With recently developed software applications, architects can calculate not only wind and solar patterns, but also shadows and heat loss in different seasons. This new software can also be used to calculate the amount of heat retained by building materials and the appliances' power consumption (Gonchar 2010). Other useful instruments include smart thermostats, which can be programmed to perform tasks, from heating less when homeowners are not in to closing the blinds on hot days (Tanha 2010). Finally, TED (The Energy Detective) is an appliance that can monitor electricity consumption and production and encourage energy saving (City of Vancouver 2010).

DRIVING FORCES

- High energy costs
- Need to reduce the home's carbon footprint
- Technological advances in the field of energy
- Cost-efficient technology

INNOVATIONS

- Low-cost energy-producing technologies
- Proliferation of photovoltaic panels (PV)
- Digital monitoring devices
- Better insulation materials and techniques

11.1 NET-ZERO DWELLINGS

Project	Lighthouse
Location	Watford, England
Architect	Sheppard Robson

The United Kingdom is one of the world's leaders in environmental design and the use of corresponding technologies. Actions and targets were set by its government to create carbon-neutral developments. Designed by architecture firm Sheppard Robson, the Lighthouse project has been acknowledged as one of the first net-zero houses in the U.K.

Built in collaboration with the engineering firm ARUP, the Lighthouse includes not only sustainable technologies, but also design concepts that raise awareness of sustainability and foster behavioural changes among its occupants. The floor area is 93 m² (1,001 sq ft), on two-and-a-half storeys. The living spaces and the kitchen, which are mostly used during the day, were placed on the first floor to receive the maximum

Below: To limit heat loss, the walls of the Lighthouse were constructed with high performance insulated panels.

amount of daylight. The bedrooms are located on the ground floor, where they are exposed to minimal light due to their low use during the daytime.

The living areas and the kitchen are top-lit by an opening, which is also used as a wind catcher and light funnel. By placing the stairs right below the wind catcher, the architect ensured that both natural light and ventilation reach the ground floor. The side windows take advantage of balconies and overhangs to reflect solar heat in the summer. To improve insulation, the house was conceived with a glazing ratio of 18 per cent in relation to the total wall area, as opposed to the 25 to 30 per cent in a conventional dwelling. Therefore, the triple-glazed windows are placed where the most-used spaces, such as the kitchen and living room, are located. To further limit heat loss, walls are constructed using high-performance insulated panels.

Top: The facades are clad with wood to minimize the houses' carbon footprint.

Left: Smaller than usual patio doors were used to reduce heat loss.

A timber portal frame that carries the loads to the foundations supports the interior spaces. Without any excavation or the building of conventional slabs, the architect created a piled foundation for the house to sit on.

The 40-degree pitched roof is covered by photovoltaic (PV) panels for the generation of power. In addition, green technologies incorporated into the building include a biomass boiler, a rainwater collection system, water-efficient appliances and phase-changing materials that absorb heat during the day and release it at night.

The house design also includes an energy monitoring system to provide the occupants with a constant feedback on resource consumption, which helps them to remain aware of their environmental responsibility. With almost no impact on the local environment and utility resources, the architect sets a framework for the net-zero lifestyle for the occupants as well as for other designers.

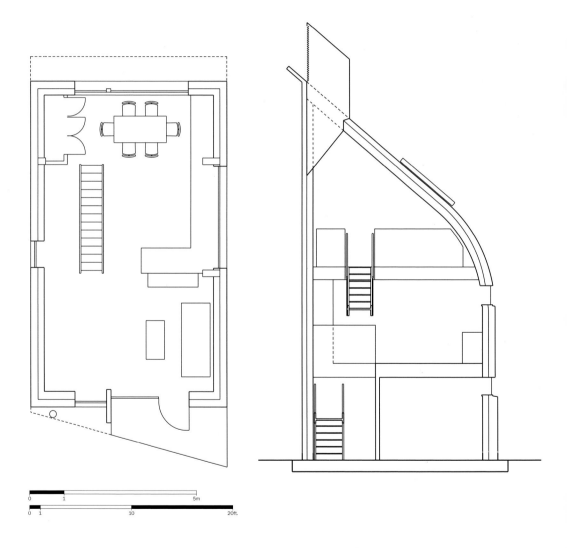

Left: The 40-degree pitched roof is covered with photovoltaic (PV) panels.

Opposite page, left: The ground floor open plan of the Lighthouse.

Opposite page, right: A timber portal frame that carries the load to the foundation supports the interior space.

11.2 NET-ZERO DWELLINGS

Project   Sunlighthouse

Location   Pressroom, Austria

Architect   Hein-Troy Architects

Austria lies in a cold, mountainous climate zone where westerly winds dominate. While low temperatures occur in the winter, infrastructures and buildings must constantly adapt to rapid weather change, which is affected by three different European weather systems. The region was intentionally selected by the Velux Corporation to host a housing competition to demonstrate sustainable design practices that balance energy and the environment. Hein–Troy's winning entry, Sunlighthouse, which was completed in 2010, has been recognized as the first net-zero house in Austria.

The design takes advantage of the sunlight around the three-level home to achieve zero carbon emissions. The house is constructed from materials that were selected due to their low environmental impact and low embodied energy. Interior walls are elegantly finished with locally harvested pine and special cement called Slagstar, which produces 90 per cent less CO_2 emissions than conventional Portland concrete, was also used.

During the warmer months,

Above: The Sunlighthouse was the first net-zero house in Austria.

Opposite page, top: The interior walls are finished with locally-harvested timber.

Opposite page, bottom: The materials for the dwelling have been chosen due to low embodied energy.

passive ventilation is induced by a 'chimney effect', whereby indoor air from the ground floor is carried to the other two levels through the house's open stairways, and finally leaves the house from a rooftop opening.

The large south-orientated, sloped roof maximizes the home's solar exposure with three different integrated technologies: a grid of skylights designed with passive solar gain techniques, allowing a great amount of natural light and heat to enter the living spaces; rows of solar thermal collectors that are used for water heating, connected to the water storage tank; and finally, a total area of 48 m² (517 sq ft) of photovoltaic panels, which have the potential to provide one third of the electricity needed by the occupants. In addition to the reduced electrical consumption, the walls are insulated with cellulose, a by-product of recycled paper.

Within 30 years of its completion, the house is projected to generate enough energy to balance the CO_2 emissions generated by its construction, including material productions, transportation and waste disposals.

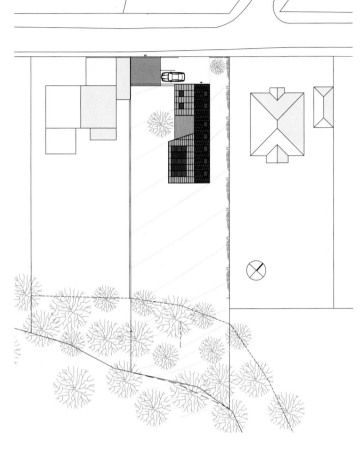

Above: Solar water heaters are noticeable on the south-orientated sloped roof on this site plan.

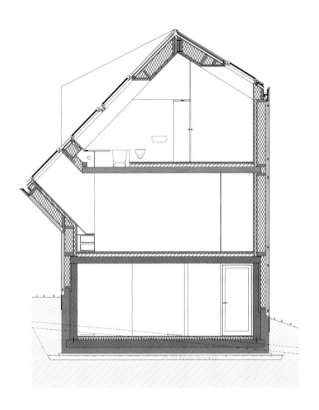

Left: A section through the skylights.

Below left: Energy- and ventilation-enhancing features are shown in this cross-section.

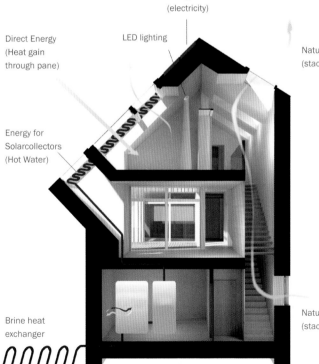

Energy for solar cells
(electricity)

LED lighting

Direct Energy
(Heat gain
through pane)

Natural ventilation
(stack effect)

Energy for
Solarcollectors
(Hot Water)

Brine heat
exchanger

Natural ventilation
(stack effect)

Chapter 12
DESIGNING FOR PASSIVE SOLAR GAIN

Dwellings designed along the principles of passive solar gain do not require mechanical means to gather and utilize the sun's energy and enhance their ventilation (Sustainable Sources 2011b). According to the California Energy Commission (2011), by designing a house to take full advantage of the sun's heat, energy consumption can be reduced by 30 to 40 per cent. Despite appearing to be simple, design for passive solar gain requires careful attention to details and application.

The two key aspects that need to be considered in passive design are the dwelling's exterior and interior. For the former, it is important to site the house properly and account for seasonal changes, solar cycles and local vegetation, while for the latter, the deciding factors may include daylight, window placement and heating requirements for each room.

During the hot summer months, a well-designed structure utilizes several techniques for passively cooling a building through either shading or natural ventilation. Shading methods may include the use of well-placed vegetation, properly designed overhangs and sun blockers, curtains and shutters. Passive cooling also extends to natural ventilation and airflow in techniques such as 'wing walls' and 'thermal chimneys', which will be illustrated below.

A passive solar dwelling must also be capable of passive heating. Once a house is thoroughly insulated, there are five methods through which it can passively gain heat: from internal

Figure 12.1: Section through a house that was designed with passive heating and cooling considerations.

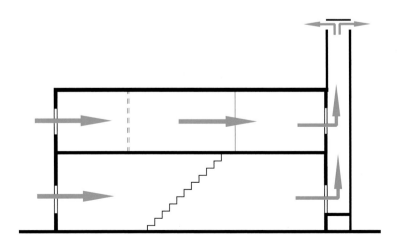

sources, direct gain, Trombe walls, thermosiphons and the inherent thermal mass, which will also be discussed below (Sustainable Sources 2011d, Tanha 2010, Sassi 2006).

A house should be orientated so that it has an elongated side facing south (or north in the southern hemisphere). Although having it face true south, rather than magnetic south, is highly recommended, the orientation can vary by up to 20 degrees off true south with minimal effect on solar input (CEC 2011). This orientation allows the building's side to gain energy between 9 a.m. and 3 p.m. during the cold season (Sustainable Sources 2011b). In summertime, when the sun is high in the sky, it still moves along a southward arc in the northern hemisphere. Situating the building to take advantage of this arc can cut the total energy usage by 30 to 40 per cent (CEC 2011). In colder climates, however, such an organization can reduce the heat load by up to 60 per cent (Johnston and Gibson 2010).

It is also important to consider topographical conditions and neighbouring structures when designing passive buildings. If possible, a building should not be positioned where a hill or a building will block solar exposure. This is especially important in the winter months when the sun is significantly lower than in the summer (Friedman 2007). To aid in calculating the shadows cast by neighbouring masses, and subsequently their effect on the design, the use of commonly available software is recommended.

Interior arrangement for passive solar dwellings is also key to achieving maximum solar input. Primary living spaces, such as living rooms, kitchens and bedrooms, which require the most heat and light, should be placed along the wall with the highest sun exposure. This wall should also contain large windows. Furthermore, to reduce heat loss from the northern facade, it is recommended that only 5 to 10 per cent of its surface should be fenestrated (Friedman 2007). Secondary or less used spaces, such as utility rooms and stairs, should be located on the north side (Sassi 2006, Sustainable Sources 2011b). Properly designed passive solar dwellings should also have open floor plans that allow warm air to easily circulate (Sustainable Sources 2011b).

One of the best ways to shade a dwelling is to plant trees or use existing trees. Planting deciduous trees blocks the hot summer rays, while allowing the winter sun to shine through. In general, leafy trees allow light transmission of 10 to 25 per cent compared to a 60 to 70 per cent when bare (Sassi 2006). Such methods not only shade, but are also known to reduce the ambient temperature around a dwelling. Natural vegetative processes such, as photosynthesis and evaporation, use up the sun's energy and prevent it from being absorbed into the building and its surroundings (Sassi 2006).

Using man-made features such as roofing overhangs can also be used to create shade. Due to the fact that the sun's rays are higher in the summer and lower in the winter, the roof can be

DRIVING FORCES

- High energy costs
- Interest in vernacular design principles
- Reduced reliance on costly mechanical means

INNOVATIONS

- New software aids in energy calculations
- Better correlation between landscaping and energy efficiency
- New glazing technologies
- Better insulation techniques and products

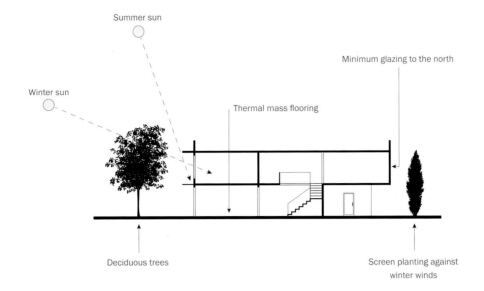

Summer sun

Winter sun

Minimum glazing to the north

Thermal mass flooring

Deciduous trees

Screen planting against
winter winds

extended to block summer rays from entering a window without blocking the winter sun (Friedman 2007). It is also possible to add shutters above windows that are too low to benefit from an overhanging roof. The same effect can be reproduced by even simpler man-made devices, such as curtains or shutters, which can be closed or opened manually when needed. Such details should be introduced to avoid heat absorption and reflect the sun's rays away from the dwelling instead (Sassi 2006).

The principle of reflecting away the sun's energy when required is also inherent in more innovative technologies such as electrochromic and thermochromic glass. Electrochromic glass, or switchable glass, is a clear sheet of glass that – with a small burst of electricity – can change opacity to become solid and reflective. Wall switches, remote controls, movement sensors, light sensors or timers are programmed to initiate the small burst of energy. Furthermore, this glass can be customized or 'tuned' to control the precise amount of light, glare and heat passing through, or reflecting off, the window (SmartGlass International 2010). This ability to customize the effect of the glazing makes it a very viable method of passively cooling a building.

Thermochromic glass is made from a thin, transparent film laminated between two panes of glass. When in direct sunlight, the glass passively turns black, or tints, according to how much sun strikes the glass. In its fully tinted state, the glass allows a transmission of only 10 per cent of visible light, as compared to its 60 per cent transmittance rate when it is in a clear state. It can take up to 30 minutes to change from fully tinted to clear after being removed from the sun's presence (Millet 2010).

Lastly, it is important to insulate the structure adequately so that any heat gained does not escape through convection or

Figure 12.2: A combination of an open-plan design and a thermal chimney can contribute to the enhancement of interior ventilation.

conduction. Having thick walls, high-efficiency low-e windows and glass doors, an air-tight membrane and a proper heat exchange system, not only prevents drafts, cold walls and cold floors, but also greatly reduces heating costs. The effectiveness of sealed buildings can be verified through a 'blow test', which can demonstrate loss of air when the building is under pressure and not properly constructed (Rosenthal 2008).

Once insulated, there are other methods through which a passive building can retain heat. Walls with a high thermal mass typically take advantage of 60 to 70 per cent of the sun's radiant energy by storing it (Sustainable Sources 2011d). It is recommended to use thermal-mass materials not exceeding 15 cm (6 in) in thickness, since heat does not penetrate more than 10 to 15 cm (4 to 6 in) into a mass (Sustainable Sources 2011d, Tanha 2010). Furthermore, for every 0.09 m^2 (1 sq ft) of glass on the facade, there should be 68 kg (150 lb) of masonry with a surface area nine times that of the windows exposed to direct sunlight (Sustainable Sources 2011).

It is also possible to gain heat through indirect gain. These systems function by placing a thermal mass between the sun and the living areas. When the sunlight heats up the thermal mass, the energy is transferred to the living space by conduction with an efficiency rate of 30 to 45 per cent (Sustainable Sources 2011d). Two such indirect systems can be used: Trombe walls and roof pond systems. Trombe walls consist of a small air gap between a glazing and a dark metal absorber attached to the facade. Cool building air enters into the bottom of the wall, which is then heated by the sun and, due to convection, rises to the top of the wall and re-enters the building via a small opening (Juneau 2011). At night-time, however, it is important to close off the air vents in the wall to slow down the cooling of the thermal mass. The other indirect gain system is a roof pond system. This consists of 15 to 30 cm (6 to 12 in) of water stored in plastic or fibreglass containers covered by glazing. The water is warmed by the sun's energy and it then slowly heats the structure beneath it. It is important to note, however, that this system may require drainage as well as structural roofing support for up to 333 kg/m^2 (65 lb/sq ft) (Sustainable Sources 2011d).

Heat can also be gained passively by a thermosiphon. A thermosiphon is a water-based solar heater that relies upon 'natural convection to move water from the collectors to the storage tank, which is located above the collector' (Johnston and Gibson 2010). The collector for the system can be either a flat-plate or an evacuated tube collector (Tanha 2010, Sustainable Sources 2011a, Sassi 2006).

In recent years, we have seen significant development of technological means aimed at improving the dwelling's energy efficiency. Bear in mind, though, that simple, age-old methods are also of great value and they need to be considered prior to investing in mechanical and often very costly systems.

12.1 DESIGN FOR PASSIVE SOLAR GAIN

Project	Trial Bay House
Location	Tasmania, Australia
Architect	James Jones/HRV Architects

The Trial Bay House was designed to allow its occupants to look out over the serene views of the D'Entrecasteaux Channel and was positioned to take advantage of the maritime climate of Tasmania: as an island between the Indian and Pacific Oceans, the year-round temperature is moderated by the large expanses of water. The house has stunning views of the plateaus, mountains and forests and architect James Jones was inspired by the aperture of a photographic lens to try to frame and capture the landscape.

As a renovation of an existing structure, the one-storey house measuring 475 m² (5,110 sq ft), is an architectural intervention that contrasts the old timber-pitched roofs with new, precast concrete walls. The addition of a new living room, verandah, courtyard and garage initiated a complete reorganization of the dwelling, which was originally built in the 1970s, and it exemplifies considerations of sustainability and health.

In the cooler seasons, when the average temperature hovers around 10°C (46°F), the concrete walls and floors that are exposed

Above: Allowing a panoramic view was a key design objective.

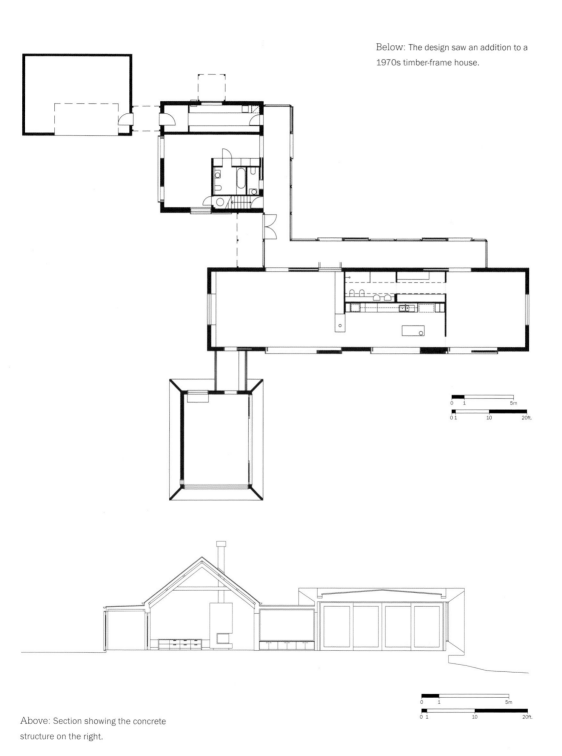

Below: The design saw an addition to a 1970s timber-frame house.

Above: Section showing the concrete structure on the right.

to the sun during the day release the stored heat at night. In the warm seasons, the precast concrete roof panels block direct sunlight from entering the interior. The double-glazed timber windows, which are orientated in different directions, are operable for cross-ventilation throughout the house.

The fact that the occupant has been a film director and a screenwriter inspired the overall design. The architect aimed to create a unique framing of the view, where the viewfinder is focused on the distant water canals and islands. For example, the occupants can experience the scenery inside the Channel Room, which is separated by a passageway from the core of the house. Floor-to-ceiling windows are strategically orientated to the north for optimal light and view.

Ecological features include rainwater harvesting and heat collection. The house is designed to collect a large amount of rainfall each season and stores it in cisterns, with solar collectors for water heating. While extreme temperatures rarely occur in Tasmania, the integration of passive design for cooling and heating creates a comfortable and pleasant living space for the occupants with minimal use of energy. The Trial Bay House was recognized by the Australian Institute of Architects with the Robin Boyd Award in the residential category in 2010.

Opposite page, top: Double-glazed patio door and windows permit cross-ventilation and contributes to energy-efficiency.

Opposite page, centre: The concrete structure on the left is instrumental as a thermal mass.

Opposite page, bottom: A close-up of the timber frame structure's interior.

Above: The Channel View room is constructed of concrete.

Chapter 13
ACTIVE SOLAR-POWERED DWELLINGS

Active solar systems employ mechanical means to generate energy, which distinguishes them from methods that include passive principles. As energy costs rise, living 'off the grid' or consuming very little power has become attractive to designers and homeowners alike. In addition, recent technological innovations have made active solar power systems cost-competitive with conventional ones, and have lowered their pay-off period to between five and 15 years (Strongman 2008).

An important part of an active solar system is its harvesting method. They can be arbitrarily sorted into two categories: those that produce electrical power and those that produce thermal energy. Electricity-producing systems are typically silent, environmentally friendly and low maintenance with an expected lifetime of more than 20 years (Strongman 2008). Common electricity-producing systems consist of photovoltaic (PV) panels, which are mounted on rooftops, within curtain walls or on separate structures. Such systems, however, are already beginning to be replaced by thin-film solar sheets, which, despite currently being less efficient than PV panels, are considerably more aesthetically pleasing, versatile and almost 50 per cent more affordable due to their ability to be mass-produced (Williams 2008, Bergethon 2011). Alternatively, thermal solar collectors are less expensive, simple and also common (Friedman 2007, Sassi 2006). They can be either water- or air-based and they distribute heat harvested from the sun. There are many applications for these systems, such as space, washing and pool water heating, as well as for cooking and water desalinization.

An important aspect of solar-powered homes is their energy storage systems. Depending on the energy collection method chosen, the systems needed to transfer and store the energy can vary greatly. Storage of electrical energy, for example, depends primarily on whether the dwelling is off-grid or grid-tied. Off-grid systems require a battery storage facility and, potentially, special appliances, while a grid-tied system requires additional hardware (Sassi 2006). Conversely, thermal energy requires a heat store, which can be located in multiple places such as the basement, a solar storage tank or even the heat collector itself (Tanha 2010, Gonchar 2010, Friedman 2007). In addition, thermal systems must also transfer the energy efficiently to the designated storage device. Various appliances such as fans, pumps and valves can aid in this transfer.

The third and final aspect to consider when designing solar-powered dwellings is maximizing energy input through proper orientation. Factors such as solar intensity and duration of solar exposure need to be calculated using tools such as sun-path diagrams to find the most suitable angle and orientation (Tanha 2010). Furthermore, a shading analysis also needs to be performed to avoid shadows being cast on the collectors from adjacent buildings or trees. In addition, solar tracking devices can be used to rotate the panels towards the sun and therefore greatly increase their input during the morning and evening hours.

A highly important aspect of a solar-powered dwelling is its electricity-producing systems. Production occurs when solar radiation excites the electrons within a semiconducting material – typically silicon – and subsequently generates direct current. The three systems that use this process are monocrystalline PV panels, polycrystalline PV panels and ribbon silicon panels, or thin-film solar panels (Sassi 2006, Quantum Solar Power 2011). For many years, monocrystalline panels dominated the market due to their durability, and they had typical efficiencies of between 15 and 20 per cent; however, newer versions can reach as high as 34 per cent (Quantum Solar Power 2011, Smith 2003).

Nevertheless, ribbon silicon panels, commonly known as thin-film solar panels, are preferable to monocrystalline panels. The wafer-thin modules are manufactured by applying layers of a semiconducting component to inexpensive materials such as glass, plastic or metal. While they only have an efficiency of 6 to 11 per cent, with experimental versions reaching 21 per cent, they are still 50 per cent more affordable (Bergethon 2011, Williams 2008, Quantum Solar Power 2011). Houses have already been constructed with solar-panel shingles, peel-and-stick wall sheets and spray-on solar sheets, which even have the potential to be applied to clothes (Lovgren 2005, Lumeta 2011, Williams 2008).

Active thermal collectors are another key component of solar dwellings that gather radiated heat. There are two types of system, the first, active air-based collectors, consist of either a perforated cladding system or a glazed-panel air-heating system (Graham 2011, Solar Air Heating 2011). The perforated cladding system is more popular and consists of dark, unglazed metal plating, which replaces the exterior wall siding. These panels have thousands of small holes through which air is drawn in by fans. When exposed to sunlight, they heat up and transfer the heat into a 1 mm (0.04 in) thick cushion of air, which is drawn into the building and either circulated through the spaces via a heating, ventilation and air-conditioning (HVAC) system, or stored in a thermal well (Graham 2011). These systems are highly effective and can reach a 60 per cent efficiency rate with temperature gains exceeding 23°C (41.4°F) over ambient temperatures on sunny days (MatrixAir 2009).

The glazed-panel system consists of a metal case with dark

DRIVING FORCES

- High energy costs
- Drop in the cost of solar panels
- Government incentives
- Technological advancement

INNOVATIONS

- Improvement in energy storage methods
- Solar panels with tracking devices
- Development of solar shingles for residential use
- Development of the evacuated tube solar method

tubes, covered by a transparent Plexiglass sheet. With the aid of fans, fresh air is drawn into the tubes and gains heat, which can then be transferred to either the indoors via the HVAC system or to a thermal well (Graham 2011). This system can have efficiencies from 20 per cent up to 80 per cent depending greatly upon the general set-up, design and factors such as air speed and air pressure (Solar Air Heating 2011). With the average payback period for both solar air-heating technologies being only two to five years, such a system is a viable method of reducing the electrical or fossil fuel load consumed by 'non-green' houses (Graham 2011).

Active water-based thermal collecting systems are more commonly used systems and comprise of either a flat-plate collector or an evacuated-tube collector (Strongman 2008, Sassi 2006). The flat-plate collector is the more commonly used of the two and consists of a series of copper tubes passed inside a glass-covered metal frame that forms an insulated box (Johnston and Gibson 2010). Such systems can reach up to 85 per cent efficiency on commercial models, with only 12 per cent of solar radiation being emitted back into the atmosphere by the panels (Bosch 2011). This system can produce temperatures up to 30°C (54°F) above ambient temperature.

The evacuated-tube collector is a more advanced and efficient technology that consists of parallel rows of large glass tubes filled with small amounts of antifreeze sealed a small central copper pipe. When heated by the sun, the antifreeze converts to steam, rises to the top of the tube and transfers its heat to collector heads before condensing back into liquid to be reheated

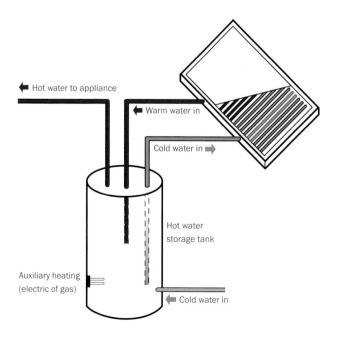

Figure 13.1: Components of a water-heating solar-based system.

(Strongman 2008, Johnston and Gibson 2010). This system is also able to take advantage of passive solar tracking due to the fact that the sun's radiation makes contact with tubes, rather than a flat surface. The flat surface has very little solar exposure during the start and end of the day because of the small angle between the plane of the plate and the incoming solar rays. This angle is known as the 'incidence angle modifier' (IAM). A rounded tube will consistently have a direct, perpendicular angle between the incoming rays which equates to an approximately 25 per cent increase in heat output performance, when compared to flat-plate collectors, solely from passive solar tracking (Solar Panels Plus 2007). Overall, while flat-plate collectors can only produce temperatures up to 30°C (54°F) above ambient temperature, evacuated tube collectors can reach temperatures of 100°C (212°F). Such efficiency, however, comes with an increased price tag, which tends to make these panels more appropriate for colder climates (Johnston and Gibson 2010). It must also be noted that most solar thermal systems are only guaranteed for five to ten years and, according to Strongman (2008), should be budgeted accordingly.

As the technology continues to advance and more efficient systems are introduced, it is becoming clear that the number of homeowners switching to solar power will only increase with time. These systems are poised not only to save money, but also to protect the environment from the harmful affects of mining, transportation, burning fossil fuels and the waste of nuclear energy production.

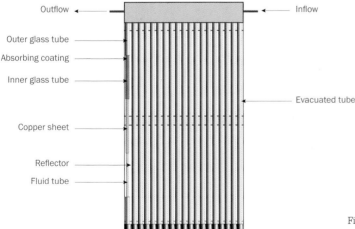

Outflow

Inflow

Outer glass tube

Absorbing coating

Inner glass tube

Evacuated tube

Copper sheet

Reflector

Fluid tube

Figure 13.2: Components of evacuated tube collectors.

13.1 ACTIVE SOLAR-POWERED DWELLINGS

Project	Home for Life/Activehouse
Location	Lystrup, Aarhus, Denmark
Architect	AART Architects

Based on the principles of Passivhaus, this house, designed by the Danish firm AART Architects and built by the developer VKR Holding gathers energy from the sun using solar means and a storage system. The home has one-and-a-half storeys, and is powered by 7 m² (75 sq ft) solar collectors for space and water heating. At the same time, 50 m² (538 sq ft) of photovoltaic (PV) solar cells generate more than the entire dwelling's electrical consumption. By producing more energy than needed, the occupants of the 200 m² (2,153 sq ft) area dwelling are able to sell energy to the local electrical power company during summer months and supplement their needs from the grid during winter when additional energy is needed. While the walls are well insulated, and the windows are mechanized for ventilation, the under-floor coil heating offers a comfortable temperature that is generated by heat pumps.

Combined, these systems create an energy surplus of 9 to 15 kWh/m² (2,800 to 4,600 BTU/sq ft) per year. Working in conjunction with one another, photovoltaic cells supplement electricity usage even when the sun doesn't shine.

The window area is equivalent to 40 per cent of the total floor

Below: The dwelling was designed based on principles of the German Passivhaus standards.

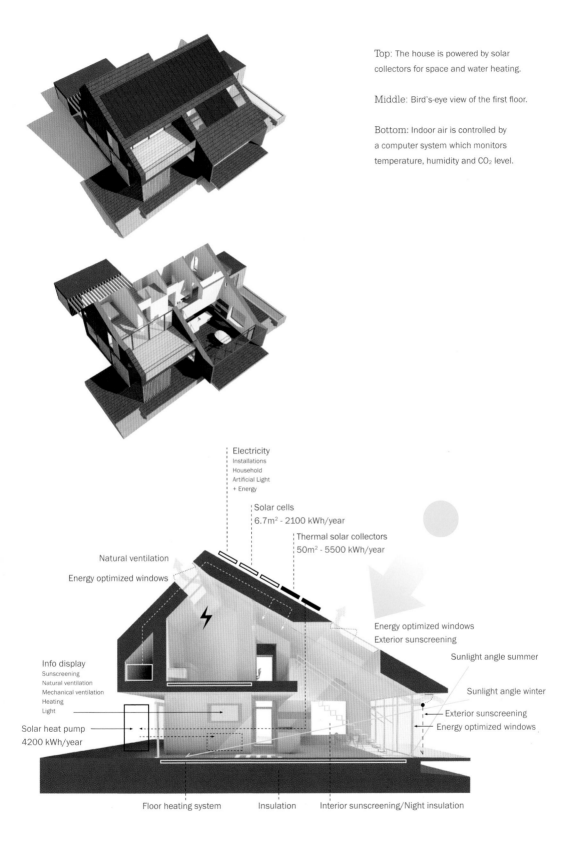

Top: The house is powered by solar collectors for space and water heating.

Middle: Bird's-eye view of the first floor.

Bottom: Indoor air is controlled by a computer system which monitors temperature, humidity and CO_2 level.

Electricity
Installations
Household
Artificial Light
+ Energy

Solar cells
6.7m² - 2100 kWh/year

Thermal solar collectors
50m² - 5500 kWh/year

Natural ventilation

Energy optimized windows

Energy optimized windows
Exterior sunscreening

Sunlight angle summer

Info display
Sunscreening
Natural ventilation
Mechanical ventilation
Heating
Light

Sunlight angle winter

Exterior sunscreening
Energy optimized windows

Solar heat pump
4200 kWh/year

Floor heating system   Insulation   Interior sunscreening/Night insulation

Top: Interior materials were chosen to foster a healthy indoor environment.

Bottom: The timber frame envelope fosters high insulation levels.

Opposite page: The high-quality windows are mechanized for ventilation.

area, which is twice the ratio of a conventional home. A notable design intention was to maximize sunlight penetration to help reduce the use of artificial light and generated heat. In addition, by having at least two different angled window openings in each room, the indoor environment fosters a healthy lifestyle for the occupants.

The construction of Activehouse followed a traditional method. The timber frame, with U-values of 0.10 for the walls and 0.07 for the floor and roof, is clad with stone slabs. Indoor air is controlled by a computer system, which monitors temperature, humidity and CO_2 levels. Windows, openings and light switches are also adjusted by the system to regulate indoor air based on internal use to provide constant and comfortable settings for the occupants.

Calculations by engineers have shown that in less than 40 years, the Activehouse will have produced enough energy to offset the amount consumed for its original construction materials and production. By that time, when the supply of petroleum runs dry and the market demand for electrical cars reaches its full potential, the dwellers will have gained enough natural energy to spare. With strong strategies focusing on long-term usability, the Activehouse is a successful integration of both the sun's energy and comfortable living.

13.2 ACTIVE SOLAR-POWERED DWELLINGS

Project	Malibu 5
Location	Malibu, California, USA
Architect	Kanner Architects

Malibu 5, a house designed by the Californian firm Kanner Architects, features both photovoltaic cells and solar water heaters on its roof. Overall, its minimalistic facade and simple geometry represent a livable and sustainable dwelling. Located on a hillside in Malibu, the house faces the Pacific coast and is strategically designed for passive and active solar gains, natural ventilation and ample views.

Essentially conceived as two interlocking C-shaped rectangles, the 200 m² (3,300 sq ft) area of the living space is powered by photovoltaic panels during the day. In fact, the building generates excess electricity to feed the local power grid.

The house was constructed from starched-plaster and concrete floors layered on the ground level. During the day, the floors act as heat storage, gaining the sun's energy and releasing it during the cooler nights. Water heaters on the roof

Top: The home is located on a hillside in Malibu, California.

Above: South facade of Malibu 5 illuminated at night.

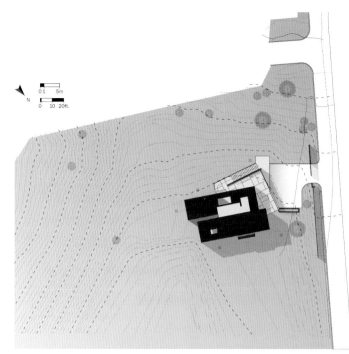

Top: The house was strategically sited for active solar gain.

Bottom: The dwelling was constructed with plaster walls.

also contribute to the radiant floor heating, providing comfortable living temperatures even during cooler days. With large openings to the surrounding views, all the windows are doubled-paned, low-e glass, filled with argon, which can be hermetically sealed to insulate the house on warm and cool days. When interior rooms are flooded with natural light, the house also minimizes the use of artificial lighting.

In addition, the design's vertical stack effect allows the interior space to have natural cross ventilation between the two floors. In the hotter seasons, passive cooling is induced by the coastal breezes and helps to lower the occupants' demand for energy.

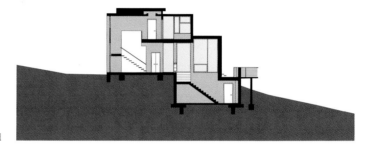

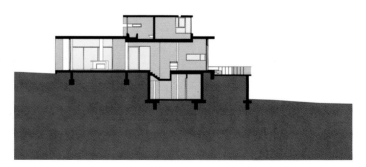

Top left: The large windows let in natural light, which reduces a need for artificial illumination.

Top right: All the windows are low-e argon filled.

Above: Section showing how well the dwelling was integrated with its surroundings to reduce its profile.

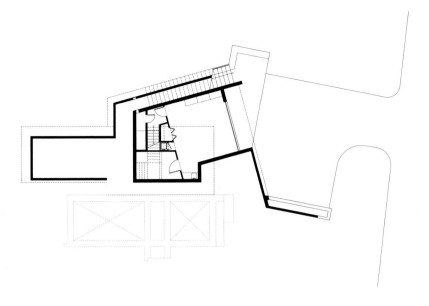

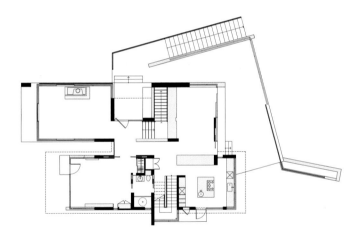

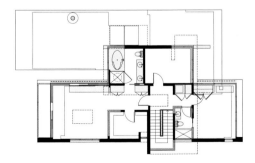

Top: The garage is built into the hill.

Centre: Ground floor plan.

Bottom: The first floor houses the bedrooms.

Chapter 14
HEATING, VENTILATION AND AIR-CONDITIONING (HVAC) SYSTEMS

Heating, ventilation and air-conditioning (HVAC) systems regulate room temperature, humidity and airflow to maintain a comfortable indoor environment (HVAC Home 2006). They can range from a simple electric baseboard heater to a complex system with ducts and lobed grilles for high mixing ventilation. Due to their importance in removing air pollutants, odours and stale air, it is necessary to negotiate balance between their cost and efficiency.

Before choosing a system it is vital to consider the size of the dwelling, its spatial configuration, its exterior envelope and the budget. Such factors can dictate the size and type of a chosen system and influence the required air velocity, temperature and energy efficiency.

For heating considerations, there are multiple air and water methods that one can choose from, such as baseboard heaters, fossil fuel central heating systems, active thermal solar heating and geothermal heating. They can be combined with others such as heat recovery ventilators (HRV) and designed for passive solar gain (Strongman 2008). For ventilation, one can choose from central duct, passive circulation and a simple ductless convection system (Stein and Reynolds 2000). These can be enhanced through the usage of the thermal chimney effect, the ridge-and-soffit vent system, grille selection, under-floor displacement ventilation and filter selection (Nastase and Meslem 2010, Sustainable Sources 2011c, Barrista 2004). Lastly, for air conditioning, it is advisable to use passive cooling options – such as natural and artificial shading, thermochemical glass, the thermal chimney effect and geothermal cooling, among others – prior to resorting to costly energy consuming technologies. Once passive air-conditioning systems are introduced, there are numerous methods to choose from for active air conditioning. They range from individual space coolers, such as window units, to central AC systems and are selected on the basis of efficiency and cost.

When choosing an HVAC system, the air-tightness of the building envelope must first be reviewed. When the envelope is highly airtight, a smaller system will be sufficient and affordable. Furthermore, factors such as indoor spatial arrangement can affect the required size. For example, if a house

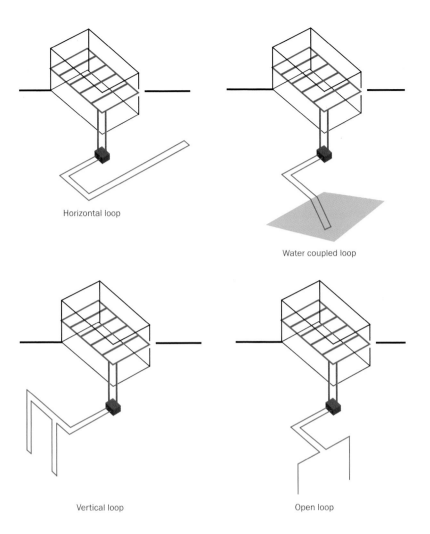

Horizontal loop

Water coupled loop

Vertical loop

Open loop

has many rooms, then a larger ducting network will be required to adequately supply and vent air, as opposed to a house with an open floor plan.

Figure 14.1: A geothermal heat pump uses the ground's ambient temperature as a source to heat or cool the home.

It is important to note that bigger is not always better when it comes to equipment size. HVAC systems that are too large for their respective dwellings will 'short cycle', causing them to fall short of their designated efficiency (AZEM 2011). Properly sized equipment, however, operates for longer at maximum efficiency and therefore creates a comfortable atmosphere by providing consistent temperature and humidity levels. Furthermore, because the average system loses 3 to 4 per cent efficiency every year, HVAC systems only last 10 to 20 years on average (AZEM 2011). Therefore, it is necessary to have long-lasting, appropriately sized equipment.

When a central heating system is chosen, it is recommended that a heat recovery ventilator (HRV) be installed (Strongman 2008). While small wall-mounted HRVs are available, they are

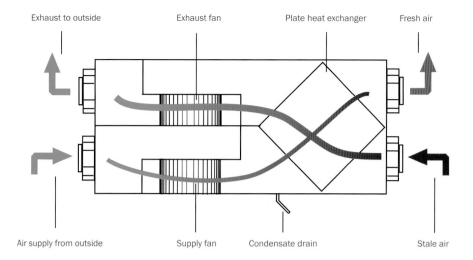

Exhaust to outside   Exhaust fan   Plate heat exchanger   Fresh air

Air supply from outside   Supply fan   Condensate drain   Stale air

Figure 14.2: A heat recovery ventilator (HRV) uses a module to transfer the heat from old warm air to cool incoming air to save energy.

typically placed in the loft and attached to ducts from centralized systems. Such a system involves the usage of a heat-transfer module, which transfers the heat from old air to cold incoming air, allowing fresh air to be drawn in with little wasted energy. This can also be reversed in the summer to conserve indoor cold air (Strongman 2008). Since this system uses energy to run the fans of the heat transfer module and central ducts, the use of natural ventilation along with passive solar heating and cooling techniques is recommended.

The chimney effect is a passive method used to naturally air-condition while supplying a dwelling with fresh outdoor air. It functions by allowing hot air to rise throughout the stairwells and vertical spaces of a house to the chimney, where it is released into the atmosphere. It then creates a vacuum, which draws in cool air through open windows placed at ground level (Sustainable Sources 2011b). This method only works with an existing or initially planned circulation route in which the air can enter near the ground and ascend through the chimney without being blocked.

A ridge-and-soffit system is a method used to passively vent air within an attic to prevent moisture and pollutant build-up. This system can be described as a 'continuous, weather-shielded opening at the peak of the roof in combination with continuous screened openings along the eaves of the house' (Sustainable Sources 2011c). This system is similar to the thermal chimney method, but is designed to function within an attic space.

The grille type for supply and exhaust vents is another part of ventilation design. For example, a stamp face grille allows only 50 per cent airflow, whereas a bar type grille allows 80 per cent (AZEM 2011). Even more efficient, however, is the recently developed lobed grille. A recent study by Ilinca Nastase and Amina Meslam suggests that using 'innovative, rectangular air-diffusion grilles with lobed ailerons ensures higher mixing in a room than baseline jets from classical, rectangular air-diffusion grilles with straight ailerons', and therefore ensures uniform flows to reduce thermal discomfort and draught sensations (Nastase and Meslem 2010).

Choice of filter is also important in HVAC systems. Homeowners typically choose the thick filters, which are known to block allergy-causing dust (AZEM 2011). These filters, however, restrict airflow and add strain to an HVAC system, which in returns requires it to run more often, using up more energy and decreasing its lifespan. Therefore, it is recommended to use thinner filters, such as 30-day fibreglass ones, and change them frequently (AZEM 2011).

Under-floor displacement ventilation (UDV) is a more innovative and efficient way to ventilate structures than the traditional overhead forced air system (Barrista 2004). Typically used in larger structures, this system lightly supplies air from 20 cm (8 in) floor vents; the air then exits the space through ceiling vents. This reduces the load on the system, which only has to condition the air where the people are, rather than trying to condition the entire space. Consequently, these systems use slightly warmer air when conditioning: 17.2°C (63°F) rather than 13.9°C (57°F). With lower air velocity, smaller fans and smaller ductwork, the overall energy and installation costs are reduced by a substantial amount (Barrista 2004).

Designers should also be aware that duct leakage is a major contributor to poor indoor air quality. Leaks in ductwork can contribute 20 to 60 per cent of air leakage in a house (Sustainable Sources 2011a). It is also known that as much as 33 per cent of a dwelling's costly air-conditioned air can leak into attics or other spaces that do not require ventilation through cracks and poorly connected ducts (AZEM 2011). Such leakages decrease air velocity and airflow efficiency, which in turn can create dangerous areas of stagnant air in which pollutants can gather.

For air-conditioning systems, it is important to choose the right size. While an undersized system may not provide adequate cooling, an oversized system is liable to short cycle, inadequately dehumidify and produce large temperature variations (REcampus 2011). To determine the appropriate size, it is important to verify the recommended area ratio, which is commonly 0.09 m^2 per metric ton (12 000 BTUs) of cooling power since the size will vary with location (REcampus 2011). Once an appropriately sized system is chosen, various types are available. If a duct system is already in place, it may be possible to install a central air-conditioning system, which, while effective, is also the most expensive (REcampus 2011). Other, simpler systems, such as through-the-wall, split, window and portable versions are available and each should be studied to find the most suitable for the dwelling's size and occupants' needs and budget (REcampus 2011).

DRIVING FORCES

- High energy costs
- Advancement in HVAC systems
- Development of energy-efficient dwellings

INNOVATIONS

- Development of advanced Heat Recovery Ventilators (HRV)
- Under-floor displacement ventilation (UDV)
- Air leak reduction in residences
- Small-sized efficient systems

14.1 INNOVATIVE HEATING, VENTILATION AND AIR-CONDITIONING (HVAC) SYSTEMS

Project	OS House
Location	Racine, Wisconsin, USA
Architect	Johnsen Schmaling Architects

Racine, Wisconsin, is an old industrial district near the western shores of Lake Michigan. Settled in the eighteen century by British colonialists, the neighbourhood has many Victorian- and Tudor-style homes; however, the bold, contemporary look of the OS House, designed by Johnsen Schmaling Architects, is not only well regarded by designers, but also by its neighbours. The home's clever integration of green technology, such as geothermal heating and advanced construction techniques, has earned an LEED platinum rating.

With an area of 177 m² (1,900 sq ft), the two-storey house was designed with proportions similar to the surrounding residences. The architects selected coloured panels and windows that infill a steel structure to reflect the wishes of the client.

Minimizing the dwelling's electrical consumption was achieved by a series of climate control techniques. The pipes of the geothermal systems were inserted 61 m (200 ft) deep into the ground; at that depth, they will remain at a constant temperature of 13°C (55°F). A total of four geothermal wells can either be cooled or heated depending on the

Below: OS House respected the proportions of the neighbouring dwellings.

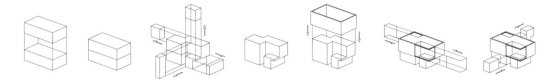

season. Since the overall design has a rectangular configuration and an open plan, it saves energy without needing to heat side rooms that are located away from the core. In addition, photovoltaic arrays and solar collectors are placed on the roof for the generation of electricity and heat.

While the integration of technical systems can be costly and visible, the architects' simple design was very thoughtful. By arranging the openings to face the water, the house has access to cool coastal breezes in the humid summer days. In addition, the inset windows use passive solar principles with overhangs that prevent the sun's heat from raising indoor temperatures. Multi-layered walls and operable windows are carefully built to ensure air tightness and a high level of wall insulation. In the summer, the facade is well ventilated due to the space between the concrete slab and the inner, wooden oriented strand boards (OSB). Installing green features can extend construction time and raise budget, but in this case the house was completed within its original time frame and budget.

The success of the design also required commitment on the part of the occupants, who were willing to make adjustments to their lifestyle. For example, in contrast with most contemporary dwellings, the OS House features

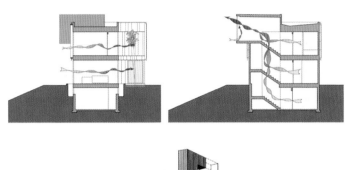

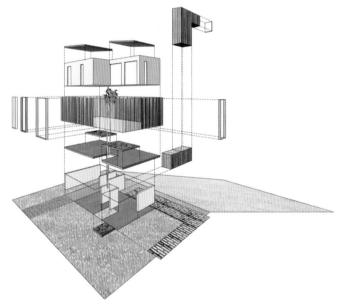

Top: Axonometric view of the dwelling's spatial organization.

Centre: The unit was designed to facilitate air flow and ventilation.

Above: Axonometric showing the assembly process.

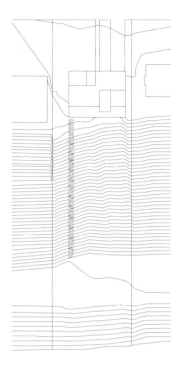

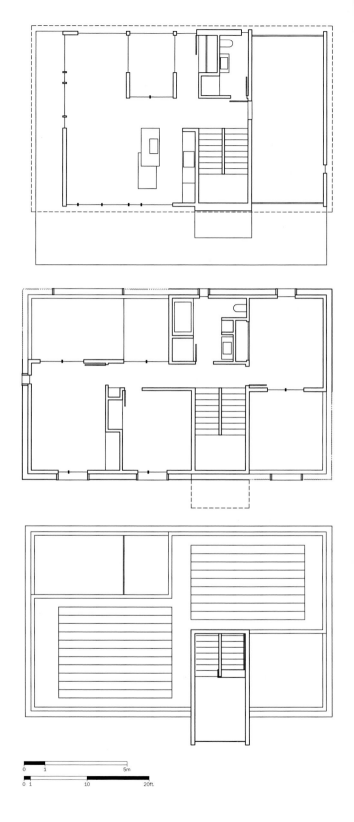

Above: By arranging the house to face the water it has access to coastal breezes.

Top right: The ground floor demonstrates the house's open plan concept.

Right centre: The second floor houses the bedrooms and has a single shared bathroom for environmental reasons.

Bottom right: Roof plan.

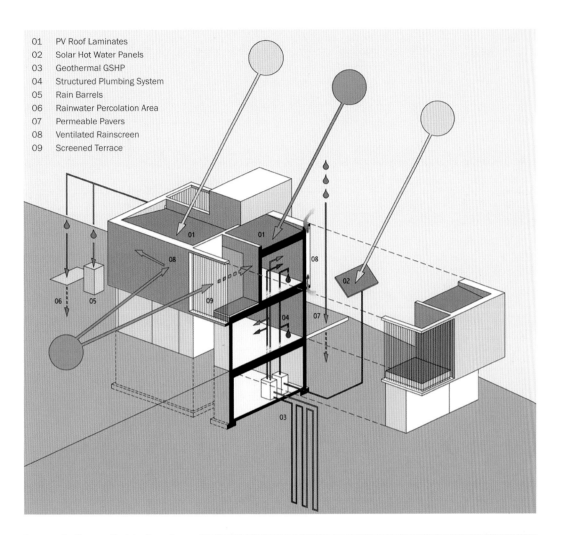

01　PV Roof Laminates
02　Solar Hot Water Panels
03　Geothermal GSHP
04　Structured Plumbing System
05　Rain Barrels
06　Rainwater Percolation Area
07　Permeable Pavers
08　Ventilated Rainscreen
09　Screened Terrace

just one bathroom that is shared by all four members of the family. Yet, with a unique visual link to the surrounding street and lake, the house presents rich, livable and elegant qualities.

Acceptance and recognition of architecture develops over time. A Merit Award in 2010 by the American Institute of Architects noted that the OS House may be a model that exemplifies a future way of building sustainably.

Top: The green features of the dwelling which earned it a LEED Platinum rating.

Above: Facade detail showing the OSB boards used for the walls.

14.2 INNOVATIVE HEATING, VENTILATION AND AIR-CONDITIONING (HVAC) SYSTEMS

Project	Pryor House
Location	Montauk, New York, USA
Architect	Bates Masi + Architects

N 0 5m
0 20ft.

Situated on a plateau at the northern end of an island, the Pryor house is surrounded by the sea and the natural environment of Montauk, New York. The architects, Bates Masi, designed the house for one of their sisters and her family, who wanted to trade city life for the outdoors. Since the clients wanted their dwelling to open to the landscape, the architects incorporated large operable windows and pocket doors. When the weather is warm, air is drawn to cross-ventilate the house, and when it is colder, the occupants can rely on their

geothermal system.

The geothermal heating and cooling system accounts for the majority of the energy. The temperature in the ground stays fairly constant at 10°C (50°F) year-round and becomes an energy supply for the house through conduction and heat exchange. In the winter, when the average temperature is below freezing, heat is absorbed by the pipes and transferred to the house's ductwork. For summer cooling, the reverse phenomenon occurs, whereby heat is transferred from the house into the ground, which is at a lower temperature.

Spatial arrangement in the two-storey house takes advantage of passive solar heat gain. The living room and the kitchen, on the ground floor, and the bedrooms on the first floor, have south-facing openings. Att he same time as integrating passive design principles, the house offers great scenic views of its surroundings. Multiple-layered bronze mesh in the clerestory windows on the second floor also provide additional shading and can be adjusted for optimal indoor brightness and desired temperature.

Far left: The house was sited on a plateau at the northern end of an island.

Below left: For viewing reasons, the house incorporates large operable windows and pocket doors.

Below: Side view illustrates the house's simple geometry.

Large floor-to-ceiling windows and multiple doors blur the boundaries between indoor and outdoor spaces. For example, a large glass door can slide open and lead the occupants into the living, dining and kitchen area from the exterior, while a smaller swinging door that leads to the patio offers a view of the ocean. Auxiliary spaces and transformations such as an outdoor shower, kitchen-turned-picnic area and living room fireplace-turned-campfire create a camp-like experience for the family.

To save time and protect the site during construction, the home was built by assembling prefabricated sections and includes 'green' finishes. It respects both living requirements and high environmental standards, and creates pleasant indoor and outdoor experiences for its occupants.

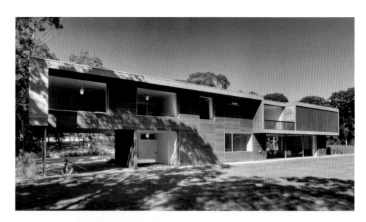

Top: The rear view demonstrates the modular nature of the design.

Above left: The dwelling's living spaces are south-facing for passive solar gain.

Above right: The living room is open to the outdoors for cross ventilation.

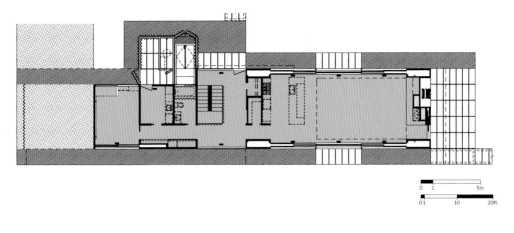

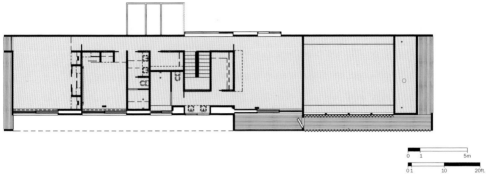

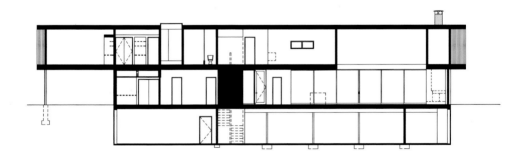

Top: The spatial arrangement of the ground floor facilitates air flow.

Centre: The second floor's bronze mesh provides additional shading.

Above: Section showing the design's modular nature.

Chapter 15
BUILDING WITH RECYCLED MATERIALS

The depletion of natural resources has made designers and builders keenly aware of the need to minimize their consumption of materials. Alongside this, another practice that has gained acceptance is using components made from recycled materials. This approach has grown in popularity in recent years, thanks to the establishment of municipal collection and recycling programmes, which provide raw materials for the manufacture of such products. This chapter describes some recycled components commonly available to those who wish to include them in their designs.

While foundations are typically constructed from tried and tested poured concrete, there are methods that integrate recyclable materials safely and durably with traditional approaches. For example, an opportunity exists to recycle materials through the choice of aggregate. Old concrete can be crushed to create high quality and well-graded aggregate for foundations. These aggregates are not only more angular, with a lower particle density than typical virgin base ones, but they are also coated with a residual cement-like paste, which increases the roughness of their surface, lowers their specific gravity and increases their water absorption qualities (Edil and Schaertl 2010).

Fly ash is another recyclable product that can be used in concrete production as a substitute for Portland cement. It is derived from combustion products at coal-fuelled electric power plants, and typically replaces 20 to 35 per cent of the cement used in concrete without adding to cost when compared to conventional concrete (Headwaters 2005, Sustainable Sources 2011e). Fly ash not only benefits the environment by using up waste, but also improves the concrete's workability, reduces water content, lowers the required time for hydration, enhances its strength, increases its durability and improves its resistance to chemical attack (Headwaters 2005, Sustainable Sources 2011e). Other recycled materials such as slag cement and silica can also be used as replacements for Portland cement (Portland Cement Association 2009).

Insulated concrete forms (ICFs), which are structurally safe alternatives to poured or breeze block wall foundations, can also present opportunities to use recycled materials when such innovative integrations are offered (Garcia 2009). Typically made from expanded polystyrene (EPS) and other foam insulation, ICFs are hollow forms that can be interlocked, stacked and filled with concrete and rebars on-site to produce insulated foundations, which are up to 25 per cent stronger than conventional poured concrete foundations (ARXX 2011). Furthermore, it is estimated that houses built with ICFs require 44 per cent less energy to heat and 32 per cent less energy to cool than wood-framed houses of the same size. They also have high acoustic insulation qualities (ARXX 2011). Two products to choose from are the RASTRA ICF and the Durisol ICF. While the RASTRA models are made from a mixture of 85 per cent recycled polystyrene and 15 per cent cement, the Durisol models are made from 80 per cent recycled wood from industrial waste bonded with Portland cement (Rastra 2011, Durisol 2011).

There have also been many innovations in the use of recycled materials for structural wood framing and interior finishes. Composite wood products, for example, are fabricated from wood particles glued and compressed together to create products that are superior in many regards to traditional, solid sawn lumber. Composite products include chipboard, medium density fibreboard (MDF) and wooden I-beams, all of which offer greater strength, longer spanning distances, higher consistency and better quality than regular lumber. Furthermore, such engineered wood products cost less and use 32 per cent more of each tree than processed lumber (Composite Panel Association 2011, Garcia 2009).

Another framing innovation that uses recycled materials is plastic wood. It is fabricated from 100 per cent recycled plastic and is substantially superior to wood products. Since it is made entirely from plastic, it can be manufactured in any required shape or size and is very durable, corrosion-resistant, waterproof, rot-proof, maintenance-free, non-toxic, UV-resistant, splinter-free, non-slip and insect-proof. Furthermore, it does not require storage protected from the elements and can be assembled, nailed or screwed into like a regular piece of solid

DRIVING FORCES

- Depletion of natural resources
- Development of products made of recycled materials
- Greater environmental awareness
- Advances in manufacturing

INNOVATIONS

- Aggregate made from recycled concrete
- Fly ash as a substitute for cement
- Insulated concrete forms (ICFs)
- Composite wood products for framing
- Plastic wood

Figure 15.1: Cross section of an Insulated Concrete Form (ICF).

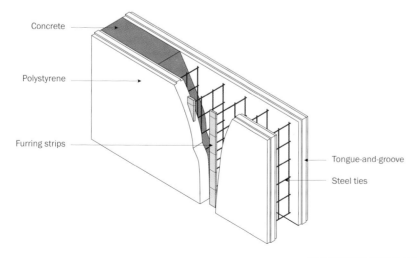

Concrete

Polystyrene

Furring strips

Tongue-and-groove

Steel ties

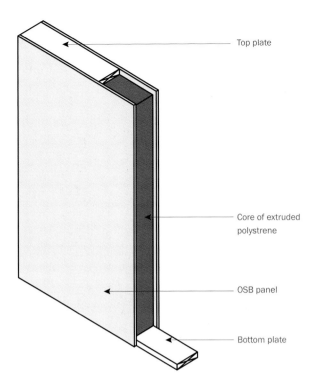

Top plate

Core of extruded polystrene

OSB panel

Bottom plate

sawn lumber. Due to the durability of these products, some companies offer 20-year warranties (Taylors 2011, Plastic Lumber Depot 2011).

Recycled framing products also extend to structural insulated panels (SIPs), which are thick panels with a core of rigid foam insulation covered by a layer of recycled materials, such as oriented strand board (OSB), plywood, fibre cement board or steel. The panels are prefabricated and customized to greatly ease the on-site assembly process. In terms of performance, they offer airtight systems, higher thermal resistance and superior load resistance (Garcia 2009).

Steel, while less commonly used in residential framing, can be made from recycled materials. Items such as used steel studs and metal shipping containers come from 67 to 100 per cent recycled steel and can be ordered to the exact required length, reducing construction waste. Despite being rot- and insect-proof and more dimensionally accurate than wood, steel studs are priced competitively in relation to wooden frames. Furthermore, their installation costs less and they can be recycled once their use has ended (SCAFCO 2009, Garcia 2009).

Exterior cladding can also be constructed from multiple recyclable products, which, after the lifespan of the building is up, can be reused. While many of these products attempt to mimic the look and texture of traditional wood siding, they can be constructed from different materials. Fibre cement siding, for example, is made from Portland cement, more than 30 per

Figure 15.2: Cross section of structural insulated panel (SIP).

cent fly ash, sand and cellulose fibres and can be made to look like masonry or stucco. Unlike traditional wood siding, which is vulnerable to fire, rot, insects and weather, fibre cement siding is durable and offered by manufacturers who are willing to guarantee it for up to 50 years. The disadvantage of this product, however, is that it cannot be recycled (Garcia 2009, James Hardie 2011).

Vinyl siding is another cladding product that offers high durability and ease of maintenance with many aesthetic options. It is primarily manufactured from polyvinyl chloride (PVC) and sold in differing profiles, shapes and colours while still being cost-effective. It is fabricated with 60 per cent pre- and post-consumer recycled content and can be assembled easily due to its embedded notches and nailing holes. After use, like other plastic products, this siding can be recycled (Vinyl Siding Institute 2009).

Engineered wood, also known as composite wood, siding is similar to the above-mentioned siding technologies. While wood–glue laminates are made from 100 per cent recycled pre-consumer wood fibres; they are not recyclable after usage and therefore only have a single life. The product is usually offered with a 25-year warranty on the substrate and 15 years on the finish. This product requires more maintenance than the two previously mentioned siding materials. The main advantage of this siding is that it is environmentally friendly due to the 100 per cent recycled products used in its fabrication (Louisiana-Pacific Cor. 2011).

Because there are plenty of materials with high heat-resistance values, for homes built with recycled materials, thermal insulation offers a variety of reusable products. Glass, plastic, cotton and newspapers can all be made into rigid boards, blocks, loose fill, rolls and Batt types of insulation, depending on R-values and local climate. Common products made of these materials and systems are cellulose and fibreglass insulations, mineral wool, cotton and spray polyurethane foam.

While residential roofing is traditionally made from asphalt shingles – which in themselves can be recycled from old tires – there are many other forms of roofing that can come from recycled products. Materials such as aluminium, plastic and rubber also exist in a form made from recycled products, and can be re-used.

With increased use, many products made with recycled content are becoming cost competitive. It is likely that sometime in the near future we will see a home whose components are entirely built from these products.

15.1 BUILDING WITH RECYCLED MATERIALS

Project	Big Dig House
Location	Lexington, Massachusetts, USA
Architect	SsD (Single Speed Design)

Top: South-east view shows some of the recycled steel beams.

Above: South-west view shows other recycled materials.

Some argue that 'one man's trash is another man's treasure'. The owner of the Big Dig House in Lexington, Massachusetts was one of the principal engineers of the American Big Dig initiative. Recorded as one of the most expensive civil engineering projects in American history, the Big Dig consisted of dismantling the elevated and congested I-93 Highway in Boston and replacing it with a central underground tunnel that changed the cityscape of Boston's downtown roadways.

The project was carried out from 1991 to 2006, and produced a significant amount of leftover materials, including reinforced concrete slabs and steel girders. The plan was to dispose of these materials in a landfill; however, one of the engineers opted to use the deconstructed materials to build his own house. In collaboration with the firm SsD (Single Speed Design), the homeowner reused over 272,155 kg (600,000 lb) of steel and concrete to build a house that measured 353 m² (3,800 sq ft).

The architects tried to use as many recycled materials as possible. To reduce time and labour, the structural elements were constructed from materials used as found; without further adjustments to the salvaged pieces. The foundation was constructed from aggregate recovered from the concrete rumbles, salvaged steel I-beams were used for the structural framing and reclaimed concrete panels were placed on the beams that formed the main floors of the two-storey house. The roof rafters were constructed using two concrete panels that had previously been used as a temporary ramp to the Boston's Tobin Bridge, and 0.69 m (2.25 ft) of grey-painted girders can be found in the roof.

Indoors, the steel framing allows for non-load bearing walls and provides opportunities for a large expanse of windows and a two-storey ceiling height. The clean and sharp volumes of the interior are 'softened' by the warmth of the eggshell coloured walls, roof gardens and the pergola over the front facade. Furthermore, the living room and the kitchen, complete with hardwood ceilings and fabric furniture, provide an intimate

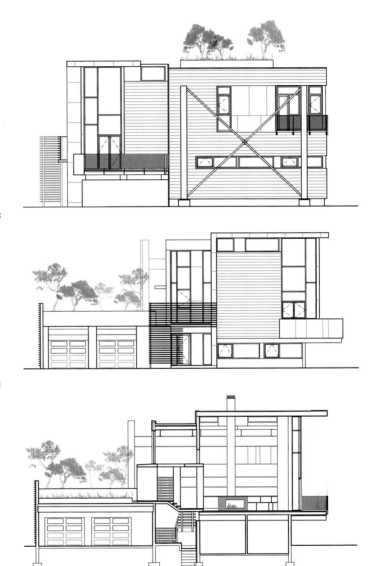

Top: East elevation showing the recovered steel components.

Centre: South elevation. The roof was constructed using two previously used concrete panels.

Bottom: Section.

ambience for the homeowners.

The project received the American Institute of Architects and Boston Society of Architectures Housing Design Award. It represents a strategic front-end planning for future public developments such as schools, libraries or offices. Recovering and reusing materials from obsolete infrastructures can save valuable resources, energy and money.

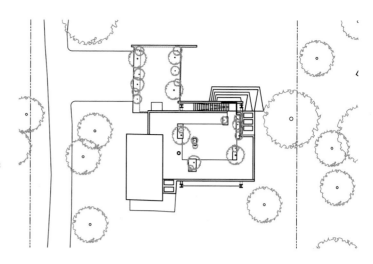

Above left: View of the mezzanine where one can see the street girders.

Above middle: View of the living room where the interior was softened with eggshell coloured walls.

Above right: View of the house from the garden.

Top: Site plan.

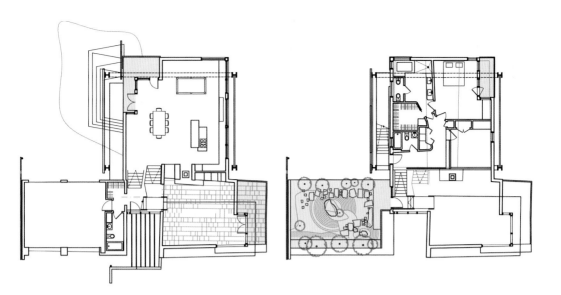

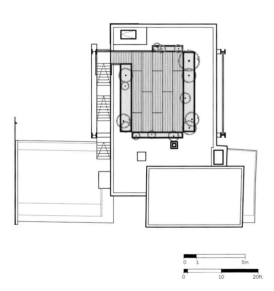

Top left: Ground floor. The foundation of the house was constructed of recycled aggregate.

Top right: First floor.

Left: Roof plan with the garden.

0 1 5m

0 10 20ft.

Chapter 16
WATER-EFFICIENT DWELLINGS

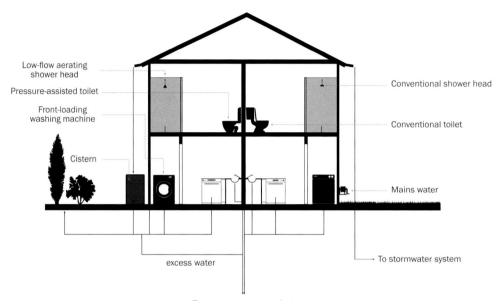

Low-flow aerating shower head

Pressure-assisted toilet

Front-loading washing machine

Cistern

Conventional shower head

Conventional toilet

Mains water

excess water

To stormwater system

To sewage treatment plant

With global concerns over water shortages, conservation and efficiency have become highly important for governments, designers and homeowners. In response, technologies that minimize water usage, and recycle waste water without compromising quality or service have been developed. Such tools are being put to use to create water-efficient dwellings.

Homeowners stand to save the most water, and as a result money, by implementing several measures indoors where over 70 per cent of domestic use takes place (Environmental Protection Agency 2011). This can be achieved by focusing on increasing appliance efficiency and decreasing flow rates. Conventional toilets, for example, currently account for 27 per cent of total water usage. That figure can be reduced by more than 20 per cent by replacing conventional toilets with more efficient models (Schaeffer 2005, Johnston and Gibson 2008). In fact, using such fixtures can lead to an overall water saving of 35 per cent in an average sized home (American Water Works Association 2010). These technologies can be applied to most fixtures and appliances found in the bathroom and the kitchen.

It is also possible to decrease mains water usage (water treated and supplied by the local authorities) by supplementing

Figure 16.1: Comparison between homes with conventional (right) and water-efficient (left) systems.

it with grey water (waste water from all domestic appliances except toilets) or surface water (rainfall or small bodies of water in the ground) (Johnston and Gibson 2008). There are a variety of systems such as cisterns and grey-water pipes that can be used to collect and distribute these alternative water sources. Despite the fact that some municipalities are hesitant to legislate for their installation due to health concerns, these systems present an opportunity to recycle and reuse water in a safe, clean way and are already widely used.

It is important that designers and homeowners review the latest water-efficient fixtures to see which will best suit their needs and budget. For toilets, there exist four common types: dual flush, high-efficiency, pressure-assisted and composting toilets (Johnston and Gibson 2008). The dual-flush toilet is highly versatile because of its two modes – one for high water conservation and another for a standard flush. The setting allows one to flush with 6 ltr (1.6 gal) per flush, which is still remarkably low compared to the many old 23 ltr (6 gal) per flush toilets that still exist in homes. The ultra-low volume mode on the other hand, can use as little as 3 ltr (0.8 gal) per flush, resulting in potential savings of up to 6057 ltr (1,600 gal) of water per year per household (Johnston and Gibson 2008). It is important to note, however, that since current technologies have produced single-flush high-efficiency toilets, which use less than 4.8 ltr (1.28 gal) per flush for all requirements, the overall advantage of dual flush has diminished and the choice between dual and single is now a matter of preference for the homeowner (CMHC 2010).

Pressure-assisted toilets are able to reach even lower levels of water usage. These toilets function by using a build up of compressed air from the previous flush to create a high-velocity flush that can use as little as 3.8 ltr (1 gal) per flush. Other pressure-assisted models function with compressed water; however, each version is equally effective, so selection is a matter of personal preference (CMHC 2010, Johnston and Gibson 2008).

Lastly, homeowners are able to reduce their water usage even further by using a composting toilet. While this may not be the preferred water-saving method for some, others have found the composting toilet to be a great tool to reduce their water usage as well as to produce fertilizer for local flora. These toilets come in a variety of styles but almost all are based upon the principles of collecting waste in a well-vented chamber without the use of water, and then turning it into compost over a period of a few months. More innovative designs can include fans, aggressive bacteria cultures and heaters to accelerate the composting process (Johnston and Gibson 2008).

In addition to reducing water usage in toilets, homeowners looking to build water-efficient dwellings should consider shower-head technologies. While conventional showers can

DRIVING FORCES

- Water shortage in many countries
- High cost of domestic water
- Environmental awareness
- New water-saving technologies

INNOVATIONS

- Water-efficient fixtures, such as water taps, showerheads and toilets
- Efficient use of grey water
- Pressure-assisted toilets
- Water-harvesting techniques

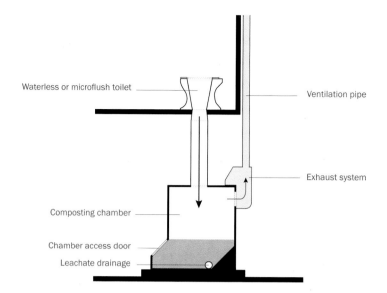

Waterless or microflush toilet

Ventilation pipe

Exhaust system

Composting chamber

Chamber access door

Leachate drainage

account for up to 22 per cent of the total indoor water use due to their high flow rates, at 15 to 20 ltr (4 to 5.3 gal) per minute, low-flow shower heads allow homeowners to reduce their shower water usage by up to 50 per cent, or an estimated 144 ltr (38 gal) per day without any loss of function or perceptual flow (Johnston and Gibson 2008, CMHC 2011b). Currently, low-flow shower heads come in either aerating or non-aerating models. Both models offer flow rates as low as 9.5 ltr (2 gal) per minute and can be bought with built-in filters that remove large particles and chlorine from the water (Strongman 2008). Regardless of the fact that they are equally efficient, however, aerating models tend to be the most popular since they use air bubbles to create higher pressure spray. It should be noted, though, that these shower heads tend to create draughts, which typically results in increased water temperature. Therefore, non-aerating types tend to have higher overall energy savings (CMHC 2011b).

Another fixture that homeowners can consider changing in order to save water is taps. While most conventional taps can be retrofitted with aerators to reduce their water consumption, it is also possible to buy them with built-in aerators. These technologies can reduce flow in bathrooms and kitchens by up to 50 per cent and can be used for most types of taps with a small investment (Harvey 2006). It is also possible to combine aerators with other technologies, such as mixer and automatic taps, to further reduce water usage (Fuad-Luke 2004).

The last category of appliances that can incorporate water-saving technologies are dishwashers and washing machines. For dishwashers, it is recommended that homeowners purchase high-efficiency models recognized by organizations such as the Energy Saving Trust. It is also important to choose appliances with water-saving controls (Johnston and Gibson 2008). For laundry, front-loading machines are slightly more efficient in

Figure 16.2: A section through a composting toilet.

energy and water consumption than top loaders.

With regard to the overall plumbing system, many distribution networks deliver water at twice the required pressure for appliances and taps to function. Therefore, homeowners can save water without loss of function by reducing rates through restrictors and pressure-reducing valves (EPA 2011, CMHC 2011b). Flow restrictors can be applied to individual taps to reduce the water flow while pressure-reducing valves are installed at the water mains to reduce overall pressure (Johnston and Gibson 2008, EPA 2011). These two systems should be balanced so that kitchen tap flow rates are less than 7.6 ltr (2 gal) per minute and bathroom tap flow rates are under 5.7 ltr (1.5 gal) per minute (Johnston and Gibson 2008).

Rather than merely reducing the water used from the mains, current technologies allow homeowners to go a step further by using alternative water sources. While many of these technologies are still being tested, or are in the approval stage, there are a select few systems that can be used safely right now. Cisterns allow homeowners to collect and distribute up to 1.42 ltr (0.375 gal) of rainwater per $0.09m^2$ (1 sq ft) of the catchment's area, per 2.5 cm (1 in) of rain fallen (Keeler and Burke 2009). This collected water can easily be used for outdoor watering purposes or indoor water usage depending on one's location. While some cities or regions – such as Portland, Oregon and parts of Australia – have adapted regulations and offer permits to allow the use of rainwater for non-potable indoor purposes, such as flushing toilets, many urban areas are still lacking the plumbing regulations to allow such installations (City of Portland 2011, Australian Bureau of Statistics 2007). If such a system is allowed, both gravity and mechanically driven distribution models exist. Each has different advantages and the homeowner's needs and budget should be weighed when choosing the most efficient version (REUK 2008).

It's possible to use grey water harvesting and recycling to reduce water consumption. These systems take grey water from the shower, sinks and laundry and use it to either flush toilets or irrigate outdoor vegetation (Johnston and Gibson 2008). In Australia, for example, between 20 and 25 per cent of households have already had grey water systems installed for many years, which have functioned properly and allowed for a significant reduction in the use of potable water. Almost one quarter of all households collect grey water for use in laundry, while one fifth use it in the toilet (Australian Bureau of Statistics 2007).

Beyond technologies, it must be noted that homeowner habits are a pivotal factor in the reduction of water usage. Those who are aware of waste choose showers instead of baths, and actively engage in installing and using water-efficient means. It is even possible to install an indoor meter to allow users to check their water consumption for which, in most countries, they also have to pay (Shirley-Smith and Butler 2007).

16.1 WATER-EFFICIENT DWELLINGS

Project	Villa 4.0
Location	Hilversum, The Netherlands
Architect	Dick van Gameren Architect

An old, hexagon-shaped bungalow, located in the outskirts of Hilversum, in the Netherlands, has undergone its fourth renovation – to become Villa 4.0. The noted Dutch architect, Dick van Gameren, carried out an innovative upgrade of the dwelling, transforming it into a beautiful and modern villa that is particularly 'green' and sustainable. The homeowners had recently completed an around-the-world sailing trip when they commissioned van Gameren to renovate their house. Influenced by the lifestyle aboard the ship, where resources are limited and need to be carefully planned ahead, the family wanted their house on land to reflect an environmentally-conscious lifestyle as well.

Van Gameren's design successfully accomplished the homeowners' eco-friendly objectives, featuring various sustainable strategies, as well as enabling a re-establishment

Top: The house underwent several renovations throughout its life cycle.

Above: Rear view with the nearby creek to where the harvester and purified water is released.

of the house's relationship to its surrounding green plot. While the architect strove to preserve the existing house, the outer walls and roofs were replaced to achieve higher thermal efficiency. Similarly, the bedroom floors were replaced with bamboo and all the incandescent lamps were replaced with LED lighting. Such features are only a few examples of the house's new sustainable improvements, which effectively reduced its overall carbon footprint.

The designers of Villa 4.0 worked to achieve water conservation. Throughout the house, both rain and grey water are collected and treated with an organic purification system, before being released into the nearby creek. Likewise, water is commonly drawn from the creek for various uses around the house. A large accumulation of water in a cistern also acts a cooling agent for the dwelling. In the summer, a rooftop pump draws water, channels it throughout the house and then it flows back into the creek. In addition, without having to leave any windows and doors open, mechanized roof systems in the central hall and a glass sliding roof in the kitchen draw a large quantity of air into the dwelling for cross ventilation.

While the surrounding deciduous trees shade the house in the summer, the architect also equipped the roof with a solar water heater. By using a radiant floor heating system in the newly constructed concrete deck floors, all of the rooms' temperatures can be regulated independently in winter.

Van Gameren's design is an example of thoughtful consideration of sustainability in all of its components and represents a practical example of an enjoyable lifestyle that is the least taxing to the environment, in both the short and long term.

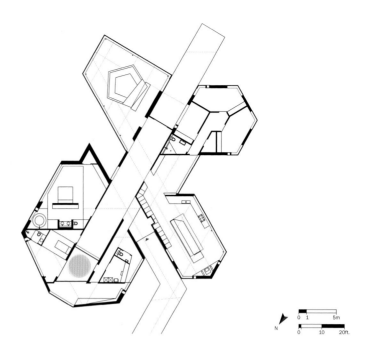

Top: The hexagon-shaped house

Right: Axonometric view showing the skylights. They also contain solar water heaters.

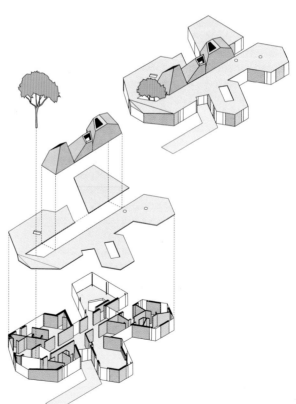

Top: View of the open plan kitchen and dining area.

Above: The entrance hallway and the other floors are heated with radiant heating.

16.2 WATER-EFFICIENT DWELLINGS

Project   7ten

Location   Venice, California, USA

Architect   GRAYmatter Architecture

Designers and homeowners in California have always been at the forefront of supporting and promoting houses that are built with sustainability in mind. Located in a popular area of Venice, California, 7ten Project, which measures 359 m² (3,865 sq ft) in area, is GRAYmatter Architecture's addition to the small collection of LEED Platinum-certified homes – the highest rating for a 'green' house – in the US. In fact, being the first conventionally constructed LEED Platinum home in California, 7ten Project was conceived as an educational model that would create a forum for discussion about environmental awareness.

Inspired by activist Ian McKellen and the film An Inconvenient Truth, developer Tom Schey was determined to build an environmentally conscious home. Indeed, the collaboration between GREYmatter Architecture

Below: Front facade of the 7ten home, where water concentration was a paramount consideration.

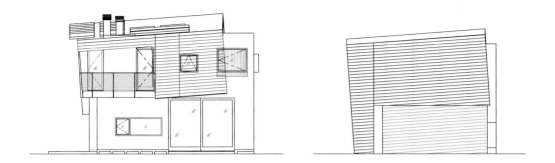

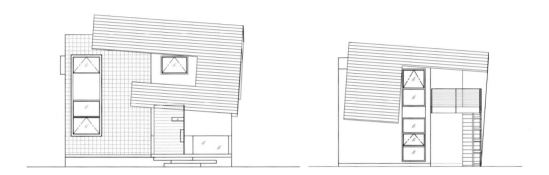

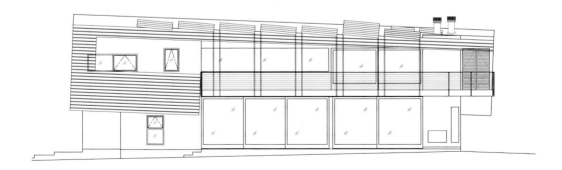

Above: Elevations of the 7ten house. The
dwelling earned a LEED Platinum rating.

and environmentalist Kelly Meyer resulted in a house that exemplifies an exquisite, cutting-edge architectural design, while not compromising the environment at all.

Every aspect of the house epitomizes the archetype of a 'green' design. For example, all the lumber used was FSC-certified, building components were locally sourced and highly sustainable and energy is supplied by solar panels. In addition, the landscaping included native species that require little water and maintenance and caused minimal disturbance to the local ecosystem.

Moreover, a particularly notable aspect of 7ten Project is its incorporation of water-efficient systems. Through effective water management – reusing, reducing and recycling – the architects aimed to make the most of every drop of water in the house. Realizing that one of the most cost-effective sources of water is rain, they integrated a rainwater harvesting system to collect and store run-off rainwater from rooftops and other impermeable surfaces. This collection becomes an on-site water supply for various water uses around the house, such as irrigating the garden and washing cars. In addition, the house also includes a grey water recycling system, which reuses indoor wash water from sinks, baths and dishwashers, for other uses such as toilet flushing. These systems effectively increase the water efficiency of the house by reducing the use of potable water for non-consumption purposes. Furthermore, other key green features of 7ten Project include Energy Star endorsed appliances that guarantee a certain degree of water efficiency. Such features work collaboratively to minimize indoor water use and achieve maximum water efficiency.

With its thoughtful and innovative design, 7ten Project demonstrates that embracing an environmentally conscious lifestyle can be simple, effective and stylish. The house was featured in the Enlightened Development exhibition,

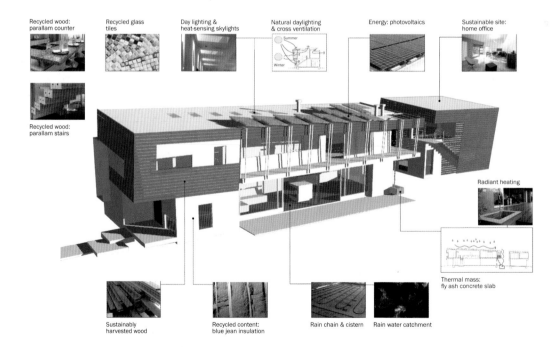

Recycled wood: parallam counter

Recycled glass tiles

Day lighting & heat-sensing skylights

Natural daylighting & cross ventilation

Energy: photovoltaics

Sustainable site: home office

Recycled wood: parallam stairs

Radiant heating

Thermal mass: fly ash concrete slab

Sustainably harvested wood

Recycled content: blue jean insulation

Rain chain & cistern

Rain water catchment

presented by the Architecture and Design Museum of Los Angeles, as a showcase of important environmental ventures and the cutting-edge development achieved by architects. 7ten Project realized Schey's objective of promoting environmentally conscious choices in everyday lives.

Top: The upper passageway.

Centre: The landscaping included native species that require little water.

Bottom: The dwelling's building components were locally sourced.

Opposite page: Every aspect of the house conception and construction included 'green' features.

Chapter 17
GREEN ROOFS

Terms such as 'green', 'eco', 'living', 'planted' and 'vegetated' are used to describe roofs where plants are used to improve performance and appearance (Snodgrass and McIntyre 2010). This age-old concept has been reintroduced using contemporary technologies in order to confront the increasing environmental challenges associated with conventional roofing. At the same time, this type of roofing can provide homeowners with financial benefits (Johnston and Gibson 2010, Friedman 2007). The types and functioning principles of these roofs will outlined below.

It is possible to build green roofs on either flat or pitched roofs. While flat roofs are the most common type, the pitched roof design is also a viable method that has been used for centuries. The common flat roof can incorporate rooftop terraces and gardens, and this version is typically more expensive due to the complex systems and membranes required to waterproof and drain water (Snodgrass and McIntyre 2010). The other version is the simpler and easier to build pitched roof, whose natural slope easily drains of excess rainwater to prevent leakage. This natural drainage enables fewer waterproofing membranes and drainage methods to be used, thereby decreasing the cost of materials and labour (Mauritius EcoBuilding 2008). While typical slopes for pitched roofs are less than 20 degrees, some companies advertise roofs with up to 45-degree slopes (Kwok and Grondzik 2007, FlorDepot 2011a and 2011b). With higher pitch models, it is important to use supports to prevent soil slippage and erosion: pre-cultivated, modular, synthetic lattice vegetation mats, horizontal strapping, battens and grids such as hexagonal lattice are all quickly overgrown by the vegetation (FlorDepot 2011b, GRHC 2009).

In addition to selecting the structure, it is also important to determine its 'intensity', or the thickness and size of the vegetation and the protective layers. This varies greatly according to the desired type of use. Those who want minimal vegetation and do not intend to walk on it can use extensive roofs, which are the most affordable. In contrast, homeowners who wish to have outdoor roof terraces, edible landscaping and trees are advised to select the intensive or the semi-intensive types.

Extensive green roofs are simple and lightweight, with little plant diversity and low maintenance requirements. Generally, they do not require any additional structural reinforcement due to the minimal substrate depth, which usually ranges between

Figure 17.1: Wooden strapping members are introduced on green pitched roofs to prevent the slippage of the growing medium.

50 and 150 mm (2 and 6 in) (Landreville 2005). This type of roof is best covered with indigenous vegetation that is resilient enough to withstand harsh climatic conditions without any human irrigation or maintenance (GreenRoofs 2011). In temperate climates, this form of green roof demonstrates the highest benefit-to-cost ratio and is the most common vegetated roof cover used (Miller 2010).

The semi-intensive green roof is similar to the extensive, with the only difference being the use of a deeper substrate, 10 to 20 cm (4 to 8 in), to accommodate a larger range of flora (Dunnett and Kingsbury 2008). This thicker vegetation serves to absorb more rainwater, further cool the roof through evapotranspiration and acts as a larger thermal mass to more effectively moderate the temperature in the dwelling (Johnston and Gibson 2008).

An intensive green roof differs greatly from the other systems by also being a garden and a terrace. These roofs typically require additional structural support due to the added weight of both people and the thicker substrate needed for the plants and trees. This substrate typically ranges from 20 to 60 cm (8 to 24 in) in depth and is composed of thicker soils and organic matter for richer growing conditions (Peck and Kuhn 2008). Due to the vegetation, an intensive roof almost always requires irrigation, fertilizing and on-going maintenance to function properly (Peck and Kuhn 2008). It is also important to note that such elevated urban spaces require safety measures such as railings and lighting (Dunnett and Kingsbury 2008).

Regardless of the type selected, to function well, green roofs must be constructed with the proper membranes and vegetation. These components serve to seal off the structure from water and root penetration damage. It is also imperative that these components provide a proper growing environment for plants by incorporating soil beds of suitable size, drainage barriers, irrigation systems and slippage prevention. Once all of these lower layers have been properly considered and constructed, it is important to select the appropriate type of vegetation. This can vary greatly according to the needs of the occupant, local climate and the type of the chosen roof. Once built, homeowners can expect a green roof to last two to three times longer than a conventional one.

While each type of green roof requires different layers and a specific set-up, their general layout and components are

DRIVING FORCES

- Environmental awareness
- High energy costs
- Advancement in roof insulation technologies
- Urban heat island effect

INNOVATIONS

- Advanced drainage systems
- Highly efficient and cost-effective waterproofing membranes
- Better structural support

similar in principle. A green roof can be constructed over any typical roofing material, such as wood, steel or concrete as long as the roof is structurally designed for the desired garden. Once the structure is set, the first membrane to be laid down is the waterproofing membrane. This membrane is the most important and is typically constructed from a material such as PVC, thermal polyolefin, rubber, polymer modified bituminous sheet membranes, liquid-applied rubberized asphalt or coal tar pitch (Miller 2010). Each material has its unique application – such as spray-on, thermally sealed layers or large rolls – and should be weighed for cost-benefit ratios. After application, it is important to test the effectiveness of the membrane with various techniques, such as intentionally flooding the roof or electric field vector mapping, which charges the moist roofing surface and looks for electrical grounds caused by contact between the moisture layer and the underlying structure (Miller 2010).

For waterproofing membranes that cannot withstand root and biological attack over the course of many years, a root protection barrier layer is required next. This is especially important for organic oil-based materials such as asphalt or bitumen, which can be broken down by roots. Therefore, it is important that designers cross reference the manufacturer recommendations of the materials used with other, regional sources such as the National Roofing Contractors Association or the American Standard Testing Methods to ensure a successful, leak-proof design (Miller 2010, Snodgrass and McIntyre 2010).

Next, it is imperative to implement drainage procedures to avoid roof flooding and subsequent, increased pressure on the waterproofing membrane, as well as potential drowning for the

Figure 17.2: Components of an intensive green roof.

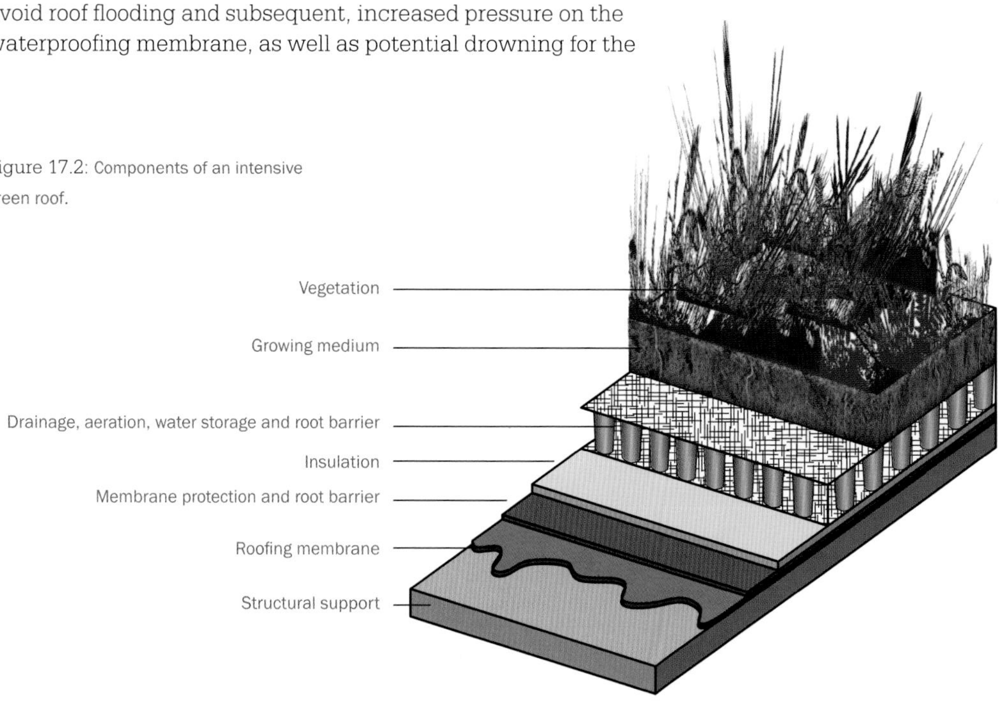

Vegetation

Growing medium

Drainage, aeration, water storage and root barrier

Insulation

Membrane protection and root barrier

Roofing membrane

Structural support

vegetation (Miller 2010). For flat roofs, it is recommended that there be a minimum slope of 2.1 cm per linear meter (0.25 in per linear foot), which leads to surface drains located halfway between structural supports (Snodgrass and McIntyre 2010). These drains and succeeding subsurface pipes, gutters and downspouts should all be cleaned regularly to prevent blockage (BCIT 2009).

Apart from having the correct slope, a green roof also requires a drainage layer to function properly. This usually consists of a layer of course medium – such as gravel – or synthetic sheets, which are not only able to shed water, but also retain some water in small depressions, similar to egg cartons, depending upon the model (Snodgrass and McIntyre 2010). While synthetic sheets are usually more affordable, less labour intensive and more effective at shedding water, there is still some debate as to whether the water-retaining versions are effective. Furthermore, there is also a discussion as to whether plants grow as successfully with it, since gravel offers root support while the synthetic sheets do not (Snodgrass and McIntyre 2010).

After the drainage considerations have been affected, the final layer of substrate or growing medium can be applied. The function of this layer is to absorb water and minerals to provide the best growing conditions for vegetation. The make-up of this layer can range from gravel and sand to thick organic soil depending on the type of roof – extensive, semi-intensive or intensive.

With the appropriate design, green roofs have the potential to offer more advantages than conventional ones. Combined with other concepts such as urban agriculture, green roofs can even be the place where food is grown (Trottier 2008).

17.1 GREEN ROOFS

Project	House Ocho
Location	Carmel, California, USA
Architect	Feldman Architecture

House Ocho, located in a nature reserve in California's Santa Lucia Mountains, offers a breathtaking downhill view of oak forests and steep meadows. Moreover, the house represents a significant achievement in sustainable design, integrating living space and natural surroundings. Designed by the San Francisco-based firm, Feldman Architecture, in collaboration with the ecological consulting and design firm Rana Creek, House Ocho received an Energy and Sustainability Honour award from the American Institute of Architects in 2007 for its use of green roofs and passive solar heating. In addition, Rana Creek also received the 2007 Award for Excellence: Extensive Roof System awarded by Green Roofs for Healthy Cities.

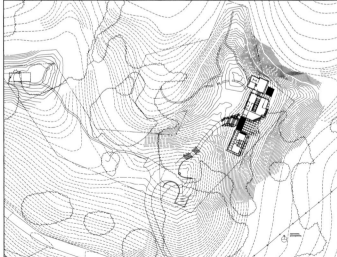

Top: The green roof, which reduced the dwelling's energy consumption by 30 percent.

Bottom: Site plan

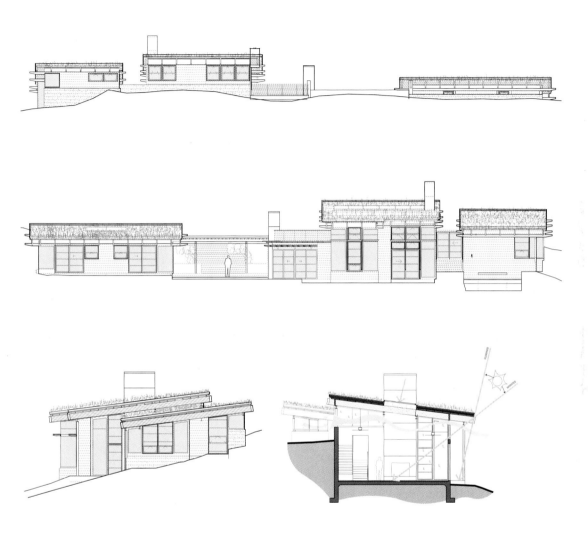

Top: The dwelling was conceived of as a series of pavilions.

Bottom left: Side elevation of the award-winning dwelling.

Centre row: Elevation showing the green roof on all pavilions.

Bottom right: The roof angle and eaves block the summer sun and lets it in during the winter.

Situated in an area with high seismic activity, the 269 m² (2,900 sq ft) house is set into the ground, minimizing the sight lines against the surrounding natural reserve, and at the same time protecting the integrity of the structure in case of an earthquake. The architects also decided to divide the dwelling into a series of pavilions to break up its overall mass and further its stability.

The most prominent feature of the house is its 395 m² (4,250 sq ft) green roof. The growing medium on the roof is 15 cm (6 in) of a lightweight soil mix, used to reduce its weight to accommodate possible seismic activities.

The landscaping around the house and the green roof consist primarily of native plants that thrived on the site prior to construction. There are flowers such as poppies and goldfields, wild berries and, other perennial plants such as Sand Sedge, Point Joe Fescue and yarrow. Rana Creek's design focused on controlling non-native species and facilitating the natural regeneration of local plants.

The green roof offers a usable landscape, filters and collects rainwater that minimizes the demand for its maintenance, attenuates sound and helps with thermal insulation. For instance, the homeowner's energy consumption in the summer months was reduced by 30 per cent due to the green roof. The roof also reduces sound by approximately 43 decibels.

House Ocho is an example of the green roof's potential in minimizing environmental footprint and in integrating architecture and ecology.

Below: The landscaping around the house includes mostly native plants.

Opposite page, top: The house is set into the ground to minimize sight lines.

Opposite page, bottom: The openness of the design offers a breathtaking view of the forest below.

17.2 GREEN ROOFS

Project   Villa Bio
Location   Figueres, Spain
Architect   Cloud9/Enric Ruiz-Geli

With a shape that replicates a sloping hillside forest, Villa Bio is a sustainable and affordable house that blends into the natural surroundings of the town of Figueres, Spain. The hilly green landscape is dominated by traditionally designed Spanish homes; however, in contrast to its neighbours, the design of the Villa Bio is inspired by natural forms and the ways in which landscape transforms and grows.

The Spanish architecture firm, Cloud9 designed the house as a ramping spiral that continuously elevates in parallel with the land's topography. Spanning across the house, the roof is integrated with one of the main sustainable features, the hydroponic garden. Due to an absence of soil, systematic requirements to prevent soil erosion are unnecessary, and the roof, covered by vegetation becomes more accessible. Furthermore, the sloping roof absorbs the excess runoff and acts as a rainwater collection system. Built without stairs, the ramped green roof was designed to be accessible for people with reduced mobility and to allow the occupants to stroll

Above: The shape of Villa Bio replicates the sloping hill side. Visible is the green roof.

Below: The design of the house was inspired by natural forms.

Bottom left: View of the hallway and stairs.

Bottom right: View of the roof garden from the interior.

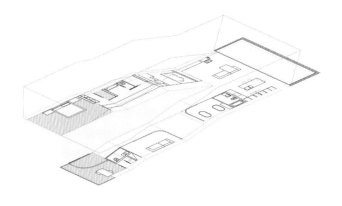

Top: The master bedroom is located on the higher half and the office space in the lower.

Second: The house is divided into two halves to create a split-level design.

Third: The dwelling is constructed with poured-in-place concrete.

Fourth: Cross section.

Fifth: The garage is placed beneath the main living area.

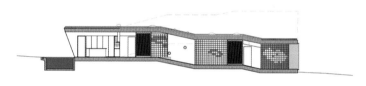

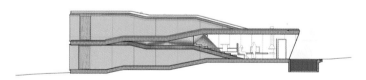

and rest on the spacious terrace.

The house was constructed with poured-in-place concrete and is divided into two halves to create a split-level design. Due to constraints created by the lot, the garage is placed beneath the house. Small openings along the concrete walls and ceilings offer multiple light sources and exterior views, while also protecting the dwellers' privacy. Without the need for support beams across the entire length of the house, natural light pours into the interior with little obstruction. The 15.2 m (50 ft) wide glass window at the rear end of the house exposes the living space to both views and light. At the front end, the master bedroom is located on the higher half and office spaces in the lower. With both spaces completed with floor-to-ceiling windows, the span from one side to the other becomes apparent.

Left: The sloping roof absorbs the excess runoff and acts as a rainwater collection system.

The relationship between a home and its outdoor spaces is an indispensable part of residential design; however, this relationship is about to become even more critical as local and global environmental pressures mount. The need to consider natural features such as orientation, topography and flora and fauna when situating a dwelling, while also benefiting from the site's architectural potential is regarded as a principal strategy for contemporary design.

Landscaping is not only about aesthetics; a garden also needs to be a place for residents to grow food and to spend leisure time. Gardens, however, can no longer be a burden on the environment. Xeriscaping can be used to help strike a balance between designing a functional garden and doing the utmost to conserve resources and the natural environment. Xeriscaping practices can reduce water consumption and the use of chemicals that are commonly used to keep lawns weed-free and green. These subjects will be discussed further in this section

Chapter 18
DESIGNING WITH NATURE

Ancient structures, such as the Greek temple of Apollo at Delphi or the Anasazi cliff dwellings in Colorado's Mesa Verde National Park, were built while considering natural features (Johnston and Gibson 2008). These principles were largely ignored in the post-World War II era; for example, when very little or no attention was paid to utilizing the sun, wind and topography to minimize energy consumption. The outcome was unsustainable residential subdivisions whose developers cleared the land and altered nature. Now turning back to sustainable practices, designers are reintroducing methods to construct dwellings on undeveloped virgin land while minimizing their environmental footprints.

When building with nature, a key consideration is preservation of flora and fauna. Constructing with minimal disruption to forests, for example, leads to advantages such as enhanced air quality, protection from the elements and storm water retention. Furthermore, having large trees around a house reduces overall energy consumption by up to 25 per cent due to both shading and protection from wind (Johnston and Gibson 2008). Retaining flora and fauna also enhances aesthetic and natural character, which in turn has been linked to improved mental health (Science Daily 2009). For designers, this is achieved primarily by avoiding unnecessary clearing of trees and the careful consideration of the site prior to construction.

Building with nature also involves the preservation of topography and natural drainage, on which plants and animals rely. Creating steep elevations with no vegetation, for example, can give rise to soil erosion or water run-off, both of which deprive vegetation of minerals, water and root support. With a decline of flora, deterioration of fauna follows, which can irrevocably change the character of a place. Therefore, planners must consider design strategies and recommend good practice before the site is chosen, during design and while construction is underway.

Another principle to consider is the utilization of wind for natural ventilation and the minimization of heat loss. The goal is to design according to wind patterns by allowing wind to enter the dwelling during summer months for natural ventilation. On the other hand, letting the wind blow into the dwelling during the winter months can lower temperature and raise heating costs. Therefore, it is important to plant new vegetation to divert wind or reduce its speed. It is also important to note that, while we will not discuss principles of narrow houses and passive solar design here (see pages 93 and 142), they are also key to the overall success and efficiency of dwellings built on greenfield sites with ample trees.

Before construction begins, it is important to plan the preservation of the local flora. Choosing a site in a clearing in a forest – or one with fewer trees – is recommended. If tree cutting is required, the site should be surveyed and a map made detailing which trees should be kept, and which ones cut. Emphasis should be placed on marking decaying trees for cutting while avoiding mature, healthy ones. The definition of a mature tree, however, varies according to the species and as such, the general size has a large range – from 45 to 100 cm (18 to 40 in) in trunk diameter measured at a height of 1 m (3.3 ft) above the ground (Friedman 2007, Nature First 2011a). When mature trees must be cut, it is suggested that they be relocated by professional contractors who can move them with up to 95 per cent success rates using specialized machinery (Nature First 2011b).

It is also recommended that areas adjacent to the site be fenced off to prevent heavy machinery from compacting the earth or accidentally destroying trees and shrubs (Nature First 2011b, Johnston and Gibson 2008). This is important because compacting the earth can severely reduce the soil's ability to retain water or air, making future growth difficult. For areas near the site that cannot be fenced off, the top 15 cm (6 in) of topsoil should be removed and stored nearby, it can then be replaced once construction has finished. This will maintain the soil's undiluted quality and internal aeration (Johnston and Gibson 2008, Abigroup 2011).

In order to preserve topography, the majority of decisions must be made when choosing the site. The objective is to

Figure 18.1: During construction, mature trees, whose circumference is greater than 45 cm (18 in) to the height of 1.5 m (60 in) above ground, need to be protected.

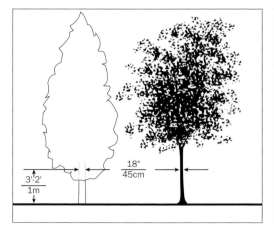

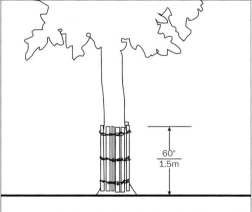

select a place in which construction will alter the existing ecosystem the least. This means that building on steep terrain, of greater than 5 to 10 per cent, should be avoided unless special measures, such as retaining walls, are put in place to prevent soil erosion, or flat areas are found in hilly environments. Furthermore, building sites should be located parallel to contour lines to reduce elevation changes and the subsequent soil erosion. It is possible, however, to construct perpendicular to contour lines with split-level designs so long as efforts are made to prevent erosion and preserve the natural drainage of the site.

Locating a building on a hill can also greatly affect its temperature. In general, all sites in the northern hemisphere should be orientated south, and should be narrow builds in order to maximize passive solar gain. Building either high or low on the slope depends upon the local climate. Building low, for example, is advantageous in hot, arid climates where cool airflow is desirable. On the other hand, hot, humid regions necessitate a high position on a hilly slope due to the need for winds to cool off the building. For cold regions, it is recommended to build at lower elevations to avoid wind. In temperate regions, it is advised to build in the middle-upper regions for passive solar gain and natural ventilation (Johnston and Gibson 2008).

It is also important to avoid altering the site's natural drainage by not adding man-made systems with sewers and storm water run-off, since they dry up the soil and put the existing flora at risk. Therefore, it is advisable to first prevent the destruction of the site's existing vegetation and then, to plant shrubs and trees where needed to retain the soil. It is also encouraged to build retaining walls to prevent water run-off from gaining too much velocity. Roadways should be designed to guide water run-off into nearby vegetation, which can absorb it to prevent erosion.

Lastly, when building with nature it is possible to take advantage of the wind to reduce energy costs. Designers should first research the local annual wind patterns to determine in which direction the summer and winter winds blow. Special consideration should be taken near bodies of water, which have strong effects on wind direction and speed (Friedman 2007). The goal with natural ventilation is to direct summer winds to blow into the home and cool it, while blocking colder winter winds. To block the winter winds, designers can use either man-made objects – sills, cornices, windwalls and fences – or natural objects, such as hills or conifer trees, which retain their leaves in winter (Johnston and Gibson 2008). For man-made windbreaks, avoiding impermeable material is advisable since it creates low-pressure zones on the leeward side of the material. Semi-permeable materials, such as holed fences and vegetation, avoid this problem and are the most effective at blocking winter winds without side effects.

DRIVING FORCES

- Environmental awareness
- High heating costs
- Increased desire for personal comfort
- Stringent environmental laws

INNOVATIONS

- Creative landscaping
- Techniques for relocating trees
- Bio swells
- Improved storm-water management techniques

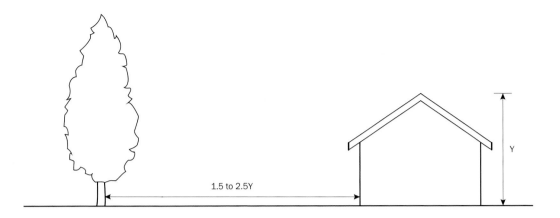

1.5 to 2.5Y

Y

When planting trees and low-lying vegetation as windbreaks, it is most effective to position them at a distance of 1.5 to 2.5 times the height of the building. This should prevent any excessive shade as well as any wind tunnels from forming between the windbreaks and the home. When the windbreak is a woodland or tree, however, the home should be located approximately 10 times the tree-to-house height ratio away from the woodland mass. For hot climate zones on the other hand, which require natural ventilation as a cooling mechanism all year long, designers should treat winter winds similarly to the existing summer winds.

As demand for housing grows, it is imperative that nature preservation principles be used to avoid destroying the environment that is in fact contributing to our lives. Building homes that integrate sun and wind harnessing technologies and topography into their designs not only benefits society in the short term, but also stands to maintain the natural beauty of ecosystems for years to come.

Figure 18.2: When using trees as windbreakers, they should be planted at a distance of 1.5 to 2.5 times the height of the building from the house.

Project   OS House

Location   Loredo, Cantabria, Spain

Architect   FRPO Rodriguez & Oriol Architecture Landscape

Located in Spain's Cantabria region, OS House is designed and built as equally 'green' as its surrounding natural landscape. The dwelling is situated along a seaside strip that consists of lush vegetation, grasses and rocky terrain. Designed by the firm FRPO Rodriguez & Oriol Architecture Landscape, the house was placed in a dug-out cavern 10 m (33 ft) from the edge of a cliff that faces the Bay of Biscay.

The building complements the downward-sloped plot on which the single-level, square-shaped house, which measures 360 m^2 (2,799 sq ft), was sited. By placing the house 9 m (30 ft) down the slope, the newly formed dugout topography causes minimal visual disturbance to the original landscape. Furthermore, the house also features a large, visible green roof. In addition to blending the house effortlessly in with its encompassing lush green vegetation, the green roof is accessible and offers the dwellers

Below: The southern part of the house is supported by pillars housing living spaces and additional rooms.

Opposite page, top: The house was placed in a dug-out cavern.

Opposite page, bottom: The house is situated on the seaside strip of a cliff that faces the Bay of Biscay.

a breathtaking view of the sea and the mountains.

The dugout topography also offers an outdoor space that protects the occupants from the strong winds and the coastal sunlight. With the floor finished in polished concrete and access to the main level and garage, the house further incorporates a living space that links the home with its natural surroundings.

The layout of the house also takes into account the location. In the northern end, the living, dining and study areas are

orientated towards the sea, while the southern part, supported by piers, contains a lounge and additional rooms.

The interior has white walls, hardwood flooring and minimal details. While floor-to-ceiling windows flood the living spaces with sufficient natural light during the day, the architects also equipped the house with artificial lights and open patios and balconies. Indoor comfort is achieved with under-floor radiant heating systems that were designed specifically for each room to optimize energy consumption. Other integrated green features include rainwater collection, which is reused for toilet flushing and watering the garden.

To protect the house from the windy and salty coastal air, OS House is clad with durable black zinc panels that mimic the

Below: Elevation (top) showing the black zinc that the house was cladded with and a section (bottom) showing the living area and the roof.

Bottom: Ground floor (left) where the living areas were oriented towards the sea. The roof plan is shown on the left.

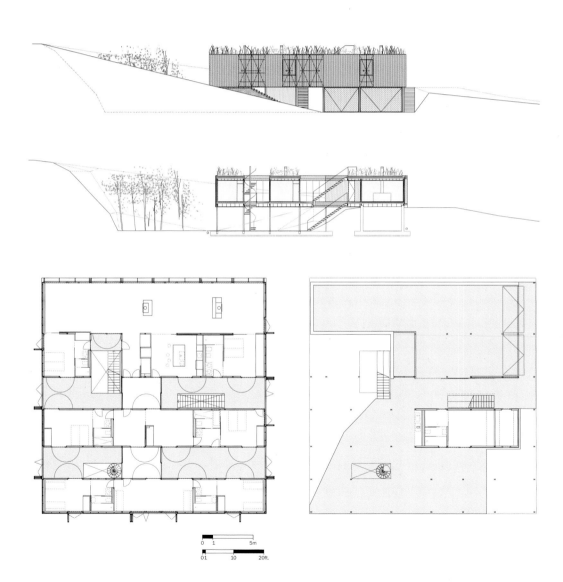

0 1   5m
01   10   20ft.

surrounding, dark-toned rocky terrain. Moreover, because the panels were prefabricated, they can be easily dismantled and replaced if need be.

The architects used eco-blocks as paving material. Their hope was to preserve the natural landscape and cause minimal impact by allowing water and sunlight to permeate while also offering an accessible pathway to the occupants and their

automobiles between the house and the street.

The design of House OS ties it to its geographical location and unique site. The integration of green technologies that protect and preserve the environment makes the house a success.

Bottom left: The floors of the house are made of polished concrete.

Bottom right: View of the upper passageway and the exterior.

Right: Site plan shows the house which faces the bay.

Project   Rantilla Residence
Location   Raleigh, North Carolina, USA
Architect   Michael Rantilla

The Rantilla Residence is in a pristine wooded site near Raleigh, North Carolina. The city is also known as the 'City of Oaks', and the region is filled with beautiful forests, creeks and rivers. As architect and owner, Michael Rantilla encountered many challenges when creating his own dwelling, which takes full advantage of its magnificent surroundings. His design responded to the required zoning setbacks and site challenges, which included steep slopes and unworkable landscapes.

The 232 m² (2,500 sq ft) residence has a height of 12 m (40 ft), which is limited by the site constraints. Three volumes, rectangular-shaped boxes, have been 'stacked' on top of one another to form three levels, in order to take advantage of the unique views and orientation. The entire structure was built on concrete pillars to minimize harm to the landscape during construction. Furthermore, the pillars prevent annual floods reaching the house during the wet seasons. With minimal

Above left: The house is made-up of three rectangular volumes that have been stacked on top of each other.

Above right: The pillars prevent the annual floods from reaching the house.

interruption to the ground below, the cantilevered rectangular volumes act as overhangs to create a number of distinctive outdoor spaces below.

During construction, Rantilla, who also served as the general contractor, managed to protect all the major specimens of the surrounding trees, which included pine, sweet gum and oak. The intention was also to let wildlife continue to live in their habitat in the forest. Moreover, the preservation of trees and small vegetation served as a privacy protection, allowing the occupants to fully experience and connect to nature in their large-windowed rooms at the rear of the house.

In contrast, the roadside-orientated facade contains fewer openings. Each rectangular volume is clad with a different material, such as aluminium and exposed concrete, to distinguish its use. Upon approaching the Rantilla house, a wooded deck on the lowest level provides a large outdoor area leading to concrete steps to the entrance. The living room on the first floor

Above: The house was constructed and sited in a region filled with beautiful forests.

Right: The second floor (top), first floor (middle left) and ground floor (middle right) offers view of the surrounding forest.

Bottom: Cross section.

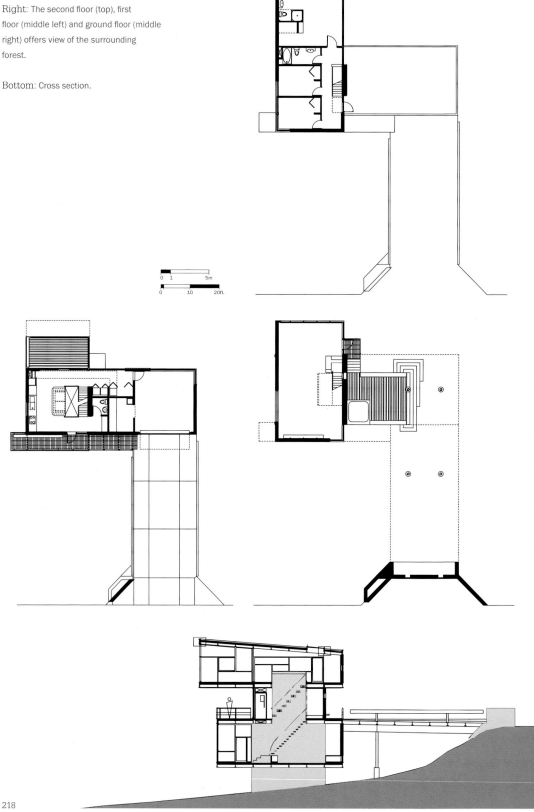

and the kitchen and dining room on the second, have an industrial feel of sorts, due to their interior décor. Some spaces have exposed concrete walls while others have exposed white metal ceilings. At the highest level, where the bedrooms are located, the floor-to-ceiling windows heighten the occupant's experience of the surroundings and the proximity to the forest is enhanced by the leaves and branches that touch the glass windows.

Determined to face his challenges, Michael Rantilla has created a delightful dwelling that embraces the natural qualities of the site. Starting from a position of preserving the landscape and wildlife during the initial construction to strategically stacking each volumetric box to take full advantage of the pristine qualities of the woodland, the house can be appreciated from all perspectives.

Below left: The floor-to-ceiling windows around the living space bring the forest indoors.

Bottom left: View of the forest from the second-floor bedroom.

Below right: A view through the various levels.

Chapter 19
EDIBLE LANDSCAPING

The desire to grow food and create attractive gardens has led to the proliferation of edible landscaping. It is defined as 'the use of food-producing plants in the residential landscape: combining fruit and nut trees, berry bushes, vegetables, herbs, edible flowers and other ornamental plants into aesthetically pleasing designs' (Oregon State University 2011). While this topic involves horticulture and agriculture, it also forms an essential part of sustainable residential development.

A thriving patch of edible landscape depends on its organization. A well-planned garden can benefit from natural factors such as sunlight and the flow of water to create a low-maintenance and high-yield plot. On the other hand, a poorly planned garden can fail, in part, from the lack – or excess – of the same factors. Therefore, each garden will require careful planning, layout and consideration of existing structures, lawn size, orientation, topography, climate and chosen plants. For example, owners of a house with a small lot might opt for vertical farming while those with a larger lot might realize

Figure 19.1: Cross sections showing optional locations for edible landscapes in a dwelling.

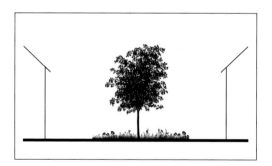

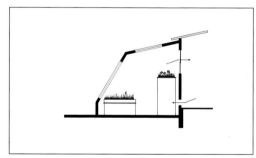

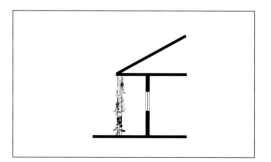

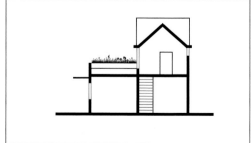

that a substantial amount of time will have to be devoted to maintenance.

Water and soil systems design all need to be considered. It is important that the needs of each plant is verified and catered to. Furthermore, the absorption capabilities, depth and richness of the soil are also critical to the success of a garden in regard to the retaining of water. With a proper design, rainwater can be collected and dispersed according to need while any excess drains away naturally.

A successful garden layout should have adequate sunlight exposure and water while allowing easy access to each plant (Kourik 2004). It is first important to know the sun path since it will define where the sunny and shady areas are. This will also influence the placement of fruit trees and vegetables patches (Haeg 2010). Next, it is important to select a planting plot within the yard area. The recommended size of an edible portion for a one-family garden varies from 55.7 to 111 m^2 (600 to 1200 sq ft) depending on how active the homeowners plan to be (Kourik 2004).

Figure 19.2: A suggested layout for a yard with an edible landscape.

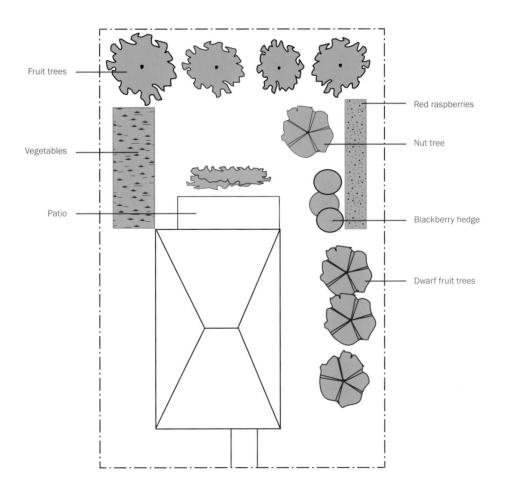

Fruit trees

Vegetables

Patio

Red raspberries

Nut tree

Blackberry hedge

Dwarf fruit trees

If the home has a small plot or none at all, vertical farming should be considered. It is most advantageous in smaller spaces due to its higher yield per unit of area. There are two commonly used types of vertical farming. The first is a simple method in which vine-like plants grow upwards using string, walls or fences (Haeg 2010). The second consists of a layered garden in which crops are planted in two or three levels (Berezan 2007). This is good for water distribution as the plants that need more water are placed in the lowest layer where water permeates slowly (Bhatt 2005).

Once the garden plot and its vertical/horizontal layout have been arranged, the pathways and crop placement must be designed. In large-scale mechanized farms, crops are planted in rows following a rectangular grid pattern to maximize output; however, this is not necessarily the most aesthetic, productive or labour-efficient option for urban farmers (Berezan 2007). Some more organic and aesthetically pleasing organizations have been created, which vary the placement of flowering annuals and perennials among paths and curved driveways. Furthermore, the grouping of plants into zones of similar water and sun needs may require more innovative arrangements than the typical rectangular shaped garden, especially if the lot is small and irregularly shaped. For example, some plants, such as tomatoes and peppers, need direct sunlight and should be placed accordingly, while other plants, such as lettuce and chard, require cooler, shaded areas (Berezan 2007). Whether the garden is rectangular or not, it is important to make sure that it is planned to allow easy access from 0.76 to 0.91 m (2.5 to 3 ft) wide permanent paths for wheelbarrow passage (Kourik 2004).

Crop rotation should also be considered during the initial design phase. While typical crop rotation in large-scale agriculture involves changing the produce in a field every growing season to avoid overworking the soil, small urban farmers can achieve the same effect through mixed-planting. This method involves planting many plants side by side in the same plot. Since each plant takes different nutrients and deposits different materials in the soil, a variety of plants will maintain good mineral balances and organic substances to avoid unbalanced soil compositions (Bhatt 2005). It is important to note, however, that only compatible plants should be grouped together. Trees, vegetables and herbs, for example, can all be zoned into their respective groups. It is also occasionally advantageous to mix zones, such as the vegetables and herbs, which can promote plant functions such as pollination (Kourik 2004). Other zones, however, such as the tree zone, are best kept separate from other zones due to the possibility of blocking sunlight and invading roots.

Beyond rotating and zoning crops, there are other decisions that must be made when selecting the soil for an urban garden. Depending on the type of vegetation and local rainfall, the levels of soil density and organic content within the soil must be carefully considered. Vegetables, for example, need moderate and organic soils. According to Bhatt (2005) 'the soil should not be extremely heavy or sandy; organic means to make the soil nutritious'. To influence these levels, homeowners can practice soil amendment. This is done by adding both organic and inorganic components to the soil to increase water and nutrient holding capacity, as well as to improve aeration and water percolation (Davis and Wilson 2005). Wood products, for example, can tie up nitrogen within the soil while others, such as peat, can influence the density and pH of the soil (Davis and Wilson 2005). The pH should be changed according to the requirements of the local vegetation. Peppers and potatoes for example, thrive in acidic soil, while most other plants need less acidic soil with a pH from 6.3 to 7 (Bhatt 2005). In general, homeowners are encouraged to research the pH, nitrogen and water needs of each plant to zone the appropriate plants together in order to maximize produce and reduce water consumption.

Lastly, a successful urban garden requires a carefully planned water collection and distribution system. Such systems vary greatly depending upon the homeowner's set-up. Vertical farms, for example, should be layered so that plants with a high water demand are on the lowest levels. Likewise, if the topography on a horizontal garden is slanted, the plants with a high water demand should be placed in the lower areas (Bhatt 2005). Other factors in self-sustaining water systems involve the collection of surface water to reduce the water consumption of a garden. A system can be set up so that rainwater from the roof of the house is redirected into plastic collection barrels, swales, berms or drywells for later usage or automated garden watering (Bhatt 2005). These systems should be programmed to water the plants thoroughly once or twice a week. This is because plants respond best to deep watering, which encourages their roots to grow downwards (Bhatt 2005).

Whether for practical or environmental reasons, society is gradually returning to urban farming. The practice of growing and transporting food from far away places is being replaced by local planting for sustainability and healthy living (Haeg 2010, City of Vancouver 2011).

DRIVING FORCES

- High food costs
- Public interest in organic food
- A desire to reduce the dwelling's environmental footprint

INNOVATIONS

- Indoor living wall
- Sun rooms with improved ventilation
- Water-saving irrigation techniques
- Vertical outdoor farming

Project	Ross Street House
Location	Madison, Wisconsin, USA
Architect	Richard Wittschiebe Hand

Ross Street House was the first home to be accredited with a LEED Platinum rating in the state of Wisconsin. In collaboration with her mechanical engineer husband, architect Carol Richard has always wanted to implement what she has learned during her career. Her own home offered a splendid opportunity to do so. The house successfully blends in with other homes in the Glenway neighbourhood, which consists of a mixture of post World War II Cape Cod cottages.

With 251 m² (2,700 sq ft), the three-storey Ross Street House has a simple design. The architect provided detailed specifications for the planting of rain gardens in both the front and rear yards. With meticulously detailed drawings for paving and the planting, the landscape was transformed into an edible and low water demand garden. Plants such as wild strawberries, western sunflower and herbs are just a few examples. Furthermore, vegetation, such as native perennial plants, which

Below: Rain gardens with edible landscape occupy most of the front and the back yards.

require minimal maintenance, also aid the occupants.

To complement the exterior of neighbouring houses and their proportions, the exterior walls are clad with 15.2 cm (6 in) tongue-and-groove cedar sidings. The exterior walls are sprayed with foam insulation and the careful sealing of the windows and doors minimizes air infiltration to less than one air change per hour. Also, to maintain healthy indoor air, the house has a heat recovery ventilation system and a three-stage high efficiency furnace.

During the design process, the architect aimed to meet LEED standards. To achieve this goal, an information model was created and computer-aided design software was used. It helped to study the amount of daylight that can penetrate the house during the various seasons. With the main southern facade entirely open, an ample amount of daylight was allowed to enter the house, while fixed louvres, strategically distanced, are

Below left: The basement level.

Below centre: First floor plan. The house has a heat recovery ventilator (RVC) and a high-efficiency furnace.

Below right: The bedroom level.

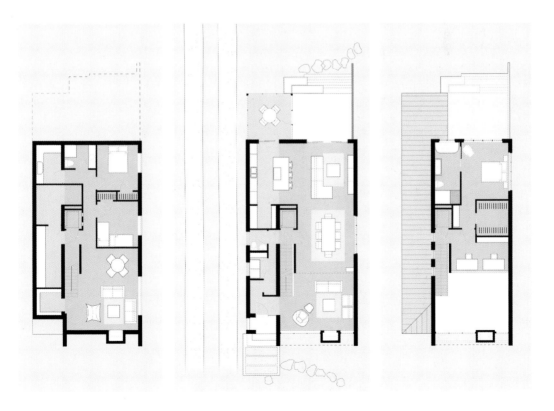

designed to offer shade in summer.

The open floor plan is finished with locally harvested materials such as maple wood flooring. The interior also has minimal details, light-coloured walls and Energy Star appliances and fixtures. Furthermore, low-flow taps, showerheads and dual-flush toilets are installed to reduce water consumption.

A central staircase, which also acts as a natural light well, connects the three storeys. The private living room and the bedrooms are located on the third floor, while the below-grade basement accommodates guests, mechanical fixtures, storage and a Belgian-style beer brewing room. The living area, the kitchen and the dining spaces are organized on the main level in-between.

While the Ross Street House integrates highly innovative green technologies without intruding on the aesthetics of the surrounding neighbourhood, the house is also very comfortable for the occupants. It is worth noting that the Madison Trust for Historic Preservation has honoured the house with the 2010 Future Landmark Award for Innovative New Design.

Top left: A view to the dining and living areas and the edible garden.

Bottom left: A view from the mezzanine to the living room which was constructed with locally-sourced materials.

Opposite: Rear garden view.

Section 4   19.2 EDIBLE LANDSCAPING

Project   Adams Fleming House
Location   Toronto, Ontario, Canada
Architect   Levitt Goodman Architects

The Adams Fleming House is located on a former brownfield site (land previously used for industrial or commercial purposes) in Toronto, Canada. While being situated near a parking lot and a vacant auto-body shop may seem like an unlikely place for a dwelling, the firm, Levitt Goodman Architects, has successfully turned the location into one that accommodates a well-designed dwelling.

Measuring 186 m² (2,000 sq ft), the two-storey house was built on a limited budget and an effort was made to economize on other resources as well. While the main goal of the interior design concept was to shut out the noise and the visual pollution of the city, the exterior includes sustainable features. The vegetable garden and a French-style orchard provide the occupants with the opportunity to grow their own edible plants in spring and summer. A fountain and an outdoor dining deck are also included on the wooden patio. In addition to the edible

Top right: The designers placed the wet functions at the core of the first floor.

Bottom right: The second floor has a study and an upper deck.

Opposite page, top: The house was built on a former brownfield site and includes many green features.

Opposite page, bottom: Rear elevation showing the vegetable garden and a French-style orchard.

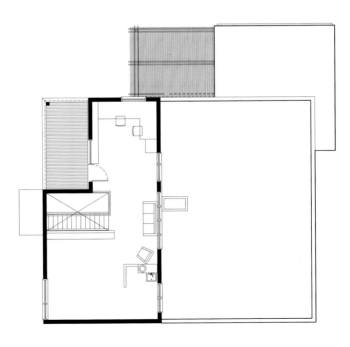

plants, other vegetation is made up of native species that require low maintenance and consume minimal amounts of water. Moreover, the roof is intended to become a garden in future and to assist in maintaining a balanced indoor temperature.

The house is organized in an L-shaped plan. Private areas, such as bedrooms and bathrooms, are placed on a raised platform, which creates storage space underneath, while the living, kitchen and dining areas are located around them. On the second storey, a large, open studio was added to accommodate the design and musical interests of the clients. Large windows flood the interior with natural light and offer a panoramic view of the garden. To save on energy, skylights and 'sun tunnels' have been used to allow natural light to permeate the central areas of the dwelling. Other green features include radiant floor and solar water heating.

The interior includes simple wooden furnishings, colourful walls and number of openings, which make the rooms seem larger than they really are. The house is also uniquely decorated with the occupants' collection of modern and contemporary paintings and furniture.

The Adams Fleming House is a successful collaboration between an architect and a client. It is also an example of integrating green strategies, technological innovations and creative ideas.

Below: Cross (top) and longitudinal (bottom) sections. The roof was planned to become a future garden.

Opposite page, top: The exterior wall contains several openings which make the space seem larger.

Opposite page, bottom left: The open plan and height of the living space helps with air circulation.

Opposite page, bottom right: The well-lit bathroom.

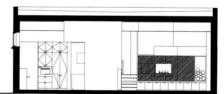

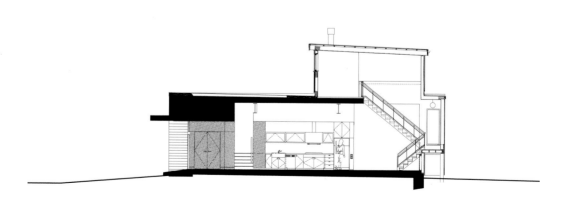

Chapter 20
XERISCAPED OUTDOOR SPACES

The core objective of xeriscaping is water conservation through the creation of water-efficient landscapes. A properly designed outdoor xeriscape not only reduces water usage by 20 to 50 per cent, but can also reduce chemical usage, requires little maintenance, and can be uniquely aesthetic (AWWA 2010, Green Venture 2011). Xeriscaping also allows for a wide range of trees, shrubs and flowering perennials to create an attractive and sensible yard.

Before planting a xeriscape garden, it is important to plan its overall organization. This involves negotiating the balance between the amount of land dedicated to turf versus xeriscaping and creating water-use zones for plants that correspond to sun exposure and take advantage of the natural flow of water. The overall goal is to reduce much of land allocated to turf, while

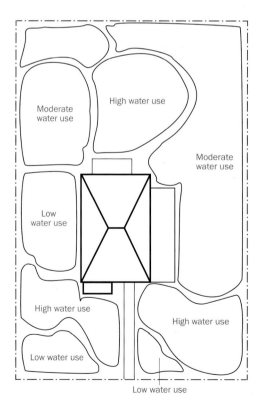

Figure 20.1: A site plan showing water-use zones.

in turn increasing the efficiency of watering. A well-designed xeriscape should be self-sufficient after its first year of growth, which will result in greatly reduced maintenance requirements in the long term (Sliva 2011, Green Venture 2011).

Once the organizational aspects are worked out, it is important to properly prepare the soil so that it can retain as much water as possible. This involves amending the soil with organic and inorganic materials, such as wood products and peat to increase both its water and nutrient holding capacity. Once the vegetation is planted, the soil will still need some attention, including the addition of mulch and proper annual aeration, to keep growing conditions suitable for the xeriscape vegetation (Bhatt 2005, Davis and Wilson 2005).

The selection of plant material is highly important in xeriscaping. Overall, it is necessary to select species that require little irrigation and maintenance. This means focusing on planting chiefly native species that have deeper roots and can survive primarily on rainwater. These species should then be located in the watering zones that were defined early on. Furthermore, when choosing turf for the non-xeriscaped portions of the garden, it is also possible to choose low-maintenance species that require little water.

Even though a mature xeriscape should function with little

Figure 20.2: Suggested landscaping for water conservation

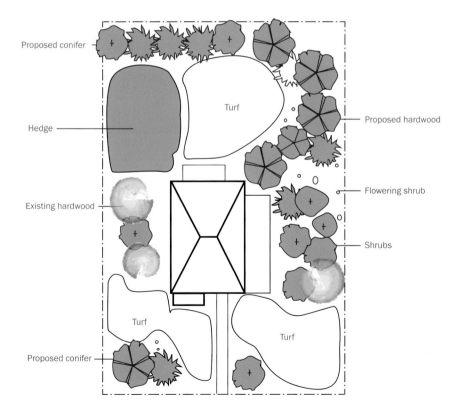

Proposed conifer

Turf

Hedge

Proposed hardwood

Existing hardwood

Flowering shrub

Shrubs

Turf

Turf

Proposed conifer

to no additional water, it is still necessary to plan out efficient systems for those plants that require more water, and for portions of the garden that are covered with turf. Efficient processes can see water delivered directly to the roots to avoid evaporation, and grey water and rainfall can be used to irrigate plants rather potable mains water (Green Venture 2011).

An initial decision that must be made in the design of a xeriscape is: what should the ratio of turf to xeriscaped land be? Ideally, one should try to reduce the amount of turf in the yard as much as possible due to the fact that conventional lawns can require up to 79 ltr per 0.09 m^2 (17 gal per sq ft) per year while xeriscapes require only 13 ltr per 0.09 m^2 (2.9 gal per sq ft) per year (Klimchuk 2008). Despite its higher water requirements, however, turf does offer a functional activity space, which xeriscapes do not; therefore it is important to retain some land for turf if needed (AWWA 2010). This means that land that is reserved for turf should only be that which is frequently used, leaving infrequently used patches, as well as areas that are difficult to water, for xeriscaping. This can include areas such as those along fences, the corners of lawns, narrow strips between the house and a sidewalk or driveway, steep slopes where run-off occurs and irregular lawns that do not fit the pattern of most sprinklers (Green Venture 2011).

The organization of a xeriscape should also take into consideration the creation of water-use zones, or hydrozoning, to add efficiency to watering and reduce waste (Kahn 2008). Plants should be clustered together into zones that require frequent watering, occasional watering or no watering at all to avoid over or under watering certain species (AWWA 2010). These zones should then be correlated with the sun path. Zones that require lots of watering should be kept out of very sunny areas to reduce the amount of evaporation from the soil and, similarly, plants with low water requirements should be placed in areas with more sunlight (Green Venture 2011, AWWA 2010). High water-use zones should be limited in size and, if possible, be placed in highly visible areas such as entranceways due to the fact that these plants tend to be more aesthetic and lush (Green Venture 2011).

The last concept involved in the organization of a xeriscaped garden is the topography and subsequent drainage patterns. Slopes which cause excessive run-off should be terraced to allow rainfall to seep into the ground for plant use (Green Venture 2011), while low spots that drain poorly should either be avoided, or amended to aid in their drainage. It is also possible to plant high water-use plants in low spots, provided it is not too wet for the vegetation (Green Venture 2011). By examining the water drainage patterns within the yard, it is possible to customize the area with backfill and redirect the water to locations where it is most needed.

Soil preparation is another important aspect of successful xeriscape design. Initially, it is important to assess the grade of soil currently in place by performing a drainage test. This involves digging a test planting hole and filling it with water. If it drains quickly, it needs to be filled up again. If this water remains in the hole for more than six hours, then the soil grade is low and should be improved for a xeriscape to function successfully (Sliva 2011). Soil grade can be improved first by amending it with organic and inorganic matter such as compost, peat and sand to achieve a soil that has high water retention, but which still drains excess water. Both compost and peat are used due to their high mineral content and high water holding capacity, while sand is needed to improve drainage and increase the oxygen levels within the soil (Green Venture 2011). It is best to mix these three compounds in relatively equal amounts and add them to the earth to encourage deep root growth (Flanigan 2011).

Once the soil bed is appropriately amended, it is beneficial to place a layer of mulch on top. Mulches are cost-effective ways to cool the soil, reduce weed growth, minimize water evaporation and capture rainwater to prevent run-off (Green Venture 2011). It is possible to use both organic and inorganic mulches such as straw, wood chips, pea gravel, marble chips and bark nuggets. Organic mulches are preferable because they decompose over the course of the year to provide fertile soil for the plants. The layer of mulch should never exceed depths of 2.5 to 5 cm (1 to 2 in) for perennials and 5 to 7.6 cm (2 to 3 in) for trees and shrubs due to decreased aeration with excessively deep layers (Green Venture 2011).

Once the vegetation is planted, it is important to maintain the soil richness by aerating. Aeration increases water retention by reducing run-off, increases the oxygen levels within the soil for better growth and also promotes deeper root growth for plants (Green Venture 2011, AWWA 2010). For thicker, clay-like soils as well as turf lawns, it is important to aerate twice a year in the spring and the fall, while xeriscape portions of the lawn only require aeration once a year due to their naturally higher water retention capacity (AWWA 2010, Green Venture 2011).

In addition to organization and soil preparation, because the overall goal is to reduce water consumption within the garden, the selection of vegetation is central to xeriscaping. It is crucial to use species with deep root systems, which in turn will depend less on homeowner watering. For the xeriscaped portions of the yard, selecting native shrubs and trees is best since they are already well adapted to the local rainfall levels, are pest-resistant and are able to support themselves in drought through more complex root systems (Green Venture 2011, Sliva 2011). Because climate conditions vary, it is important to contact local growing agencies to find out which perennials and plants will be best for xeriscaping.

Where turf is required, it is important to avoid using conventional bluegrasses, which require a lot of water, instead, choose other, hardier and more water-efficient species such

DRIVING FORCES

- Shortage of water in many regions
- Need for water conservation/ imposed water restrictions
- Environmental awareness
- Interest in organic food

INNOVATIONS

- Advanced domestic irrigation techniques
- Creative use of water zones

as rye and fescue. Many of these species are almost identical to bluegrass with the exception that they tend to be softer underfoot and require little to no mowing or chemicals (Green Venture 2011). Certain species of fescue, for instance, tend to have deeper roots than bluegrass and therefore retain their colour even during droughts. They are frequently used on golf courses, sports fields and parks due to their deep green colour and natural weed resistance (Khan 2010).

Finally, it is important to install effective irrigation in xeriscapes to facilitate maintenance as well as maximize water-usage efficiency. The best way to reduce the usage of hose water in irrigation is to obtain water through natural sources, such as rainwater run-off and grey water. Harvesting run-off water from guttering, outbuildings and paved surfaces and then channelling it into a retention pond or rain barrels can add up to 100,000 ltr (26,000 gal) of saved water each year in temperate climate zones (Green Venture 2011, Sliva 2011). This water should then be dispersed directly to the roots using a drip hose rather than a sprinkler due to the fact that sprinklers lose over a third of their water output to evaporation in the air and from the leaves of vegetation (Flanigan 2011, Sliva 2011). It is also possible to design

Below: Shredded tree mulch is most effective in reducing water loss in xeriscaping.

the water delivery drip system so that it delivers different amounts of water to different water-usage zones for maximum efficiency and minimal up-keep (Green Venture 2011).

When watering, the objective is to water deeply and less frequently (Green Venture 2010). Deep watering encourages deep root growth while shallow, frequent watering is detrimental to vegetation because it encourages shallow root growth and dependence upon the homeowner. Each type of vegetation, however, requires a different amount of water to account for a 'deep' watering. For shrubs and perennials, it is important to water to depth of 30 cm (1 ft) while annuals and vegetables only require a water depth of 15 to 20 cm (6 to 8 in). Trees, on the other hand, should be watered very deeply depending on the species. Aspen, birch and cedar, for example, are water-loving trees, which may require more than other tree species (Green Venture 2011).

Although the initial set-up for a xeriscape may seem expensive and daunting, the benefits reach far into the future. Personal benefits include financial savings on chemicals, fertilizers and water use, and less time spent on maintenance. These gardens also contain a unique aesthetic, character and message about the environment and our place in it.

Project	Residence for a Briard
Location	Culver City, California, USA
Architect	Sander Architects

To architect Whitney Sander, the Residence for a Briard is known as the first 'hybrid house', while for others, it is an integration of eco-friendly construction and affordable living that meets the requirements of its occupants. Featuring ecological interventions and cutting-edge technology, the residence, situated in Culver City, California, is a duplex that was built under a budget constraint. While the client did not have special requirements, the architect efficiently integrated systems that optimize water usage and xeriscaped gardens.

The house, with an area of 353 m² (3,800 sq ft), was constructed from cost-saving prefabricated, recycled steel frames. The pieces were delivered by the manufacturers and completed on-site to form a two-storey house within three weeks.

One particularly notable feature of the house is its water-usage efficiency. Following thoughtful site planning and design, the architects selected plants that require minimal irrigation and maintenance. In addition, an outdoor cistern was installed to capture rainwater for various

Bottom left: The dwelling is an integration of eco-friendly construction and affordable living.

Below, right: The house was constructed with prefabricated steel frame components.

Below: Site and ground floor plans showing the xeriscaped area.

Bottom left: Rear facade of Residence for a Briard. The walls were insulated with recycled denim.

Bottom right: The transparent facade lets in ample amounts of natural light.

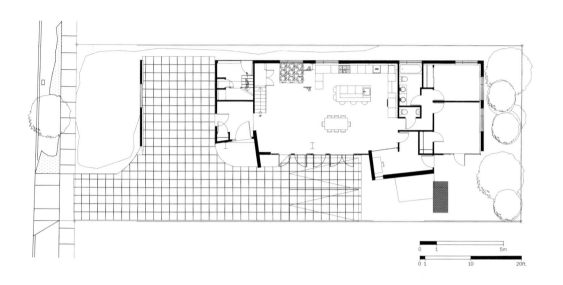

water uses, including garden irrigation. Furthermore, with a built-in grey water system, water from the sinks and showers can be reused, thereby reducing fresh water consumption from external sources.

The steel frames create special interior qualities. With the living space spanning across a height of 8.5 m (28 ft), the space is characterized by a vast amount of natural light reflecting off the crisp edges of the I-beams, hanging light fixtures and stained concrete floors. The walls are clad with green materials such as sunflower seed wallboards. The dining, kitchen and living spaces, which are organized on the first floor, face south and are connected to an outdoor terrace.

The architect also integrated ecological techniques indoors. The house maintains a constant temperature and minimizes energy use through a building envelope that is well insulated with a material made from recycled denim. Equipped with low-flush toilets, sustainable kitchen and bathroom cabinetry and Energy Star appliances, sustainability is an integral part of the occupants' lifestyle.

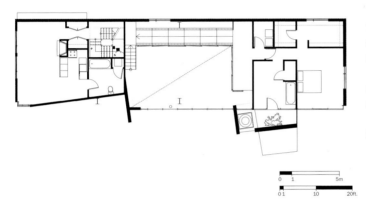

Top: The first floor shows the two sections of the house which are connected by a bridge.

Centre: Mezzanine showing the two-storey spaces.

Bottom: Longitudinal section.

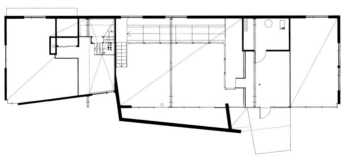

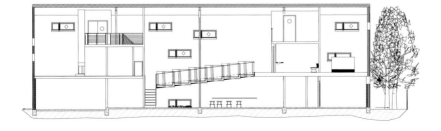

Top left: Facade detail demonstrating its transparency.

Top right: Rear elevation at nighttime.

Bottom left: Cross section.

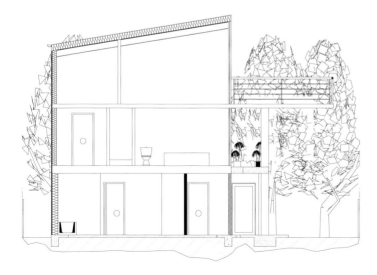

Section 4   20.2 XERISCAPED OUTDOOR SPACES

Project   Jacobson Residence

Location   Los Angeles, California, USA

Architect   Wick Architecture and Design

The Jacobson Residence, located in the San Fernando Valley, Los Angeles, is 'green' both inside and out. Designed by Wick Architecture and Design, this 372 m² (4,000 sq ft) house earned certification by both Build It Green and Energy Star for its sustainability. Situated on a tight urban site, Wick's design focused on using eco-friendly materials and being energy and water efficient. For instance, large windows in each room draw in

abundant natural light, as well as enabling sufficient natural ventilation, which effectively keep energy costs down.

While the house was built with green components, such as a basement made from insulated concrete forms, radiant barrier roof panelling and a cool roof, the outdoors was also designed with sustainability in mind. A splayed slot garden is situated in the dwelling's centre, which helps to bring natural light and breezes to

Below: The house, situated on a tight urban site, uses many eco-friendly features.

Below: Sections through the dwelling. Water harvesting features have been installed on the roof.

Bottom left: Rear view of the xeriscaped garden, which includes many native plants.

Bottom right: The permeable pavers help in storm-water management.

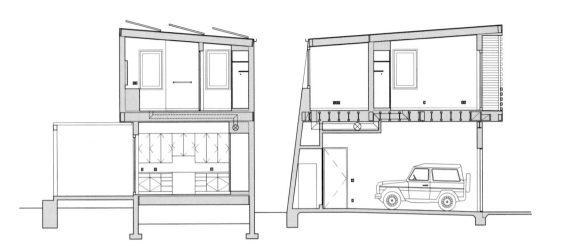

all spaces. Moreover, the central and exterior gardens both use xeriscaping techniques.

With landscape design by Fletcher Studio and rainwater recycling system by Fountainhead, Wick strategically built a roofline that is tilted in three directions, which allows rainwater to flow to a central storage tank for reuse. As a result, the occupants of the Jacobson Residence are able to collect all the rainwater, which they can then used to irrigate their garden. The use of xeriscaping enables the maintenance of the gardens on rainwater alone, significantly reducing water consumption during the dry season.

With the objective of conserving energy and water, xeriscaping has become an integral part of green home designs. Notable approaches to xeriscaping include retaining as much of the native vegetation as possible – since most is accustomed to the local climate – and placing plants in ways that optimize sun exposure, which also helps to support energy efficiency in the house. While it may require some more careful planning than conventional landscaping methods, xeriscaping can contribute to the creation of beautiful and sustainable outdoor living spaces.

Below: Ground floor features a central xeriscaped garden (left), which is also visible from the first floor (right).

Opposite, top: View of the living space, and the central and rear gardens.

Opposite, bottom left: View of the rear facade at nighttime.

Opposite, bottom right: The lower floor bathroom that contains water-saving features.

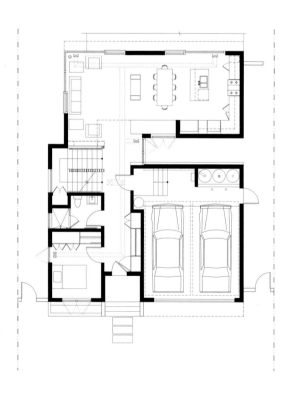

N

| 0 | 1 | | 5m |
| 0 | | 10 | 20ft. |

Bibliography

ABI Research. 2010. 'Personal Robotics Market to Top $19 Billion in 2017.' Last modified September 29.

Abigroup. 2011. 'Flora and Fauna.' *Abigroup Contractors, Melbourne Authority.* Last modified April 15, 2011.

Aisslinger, Werner. 2009. 'Loftcube.' Accessed Jun 6, 2011.

Alchemy Architects. 2011 'Weehouse: FAQ.' Accessed July 19, 2011.

Aller Air: Air Purifiers. 2009. *Home & office indoor air purifiers featuring activated carbon and HEPA.*

Arizona Energy Management (AZEM). 2011. 'Heating and Air Conditioning System.' Accessed on June 23.

Assai, Reza. 2008. *Plug and Play Homes: Self-contained Prefabricated Plug-in Units.* Master's Thesis. McGill University.

Australian Bureau of Statistics. 2007. 'Water Conservation Inside the Dwelling.' Accessed July 7, 2011.

ARXX, 2011. 'ARXX ICF Insulated Concrete Forms Brochure,' Accessed June 30, 2011.

AWWA (American Water Works Association). 2010. 'Landscaping Tips: Xeriscape, Conservation Landscaping.' Accessed July 18, 2011.

Barrista, Dave. 2004. 'Technology Takes Center Stage.' *Building Design and Construction Magazine,* April, vol. 45, Iss. 4.

Bas, Ed. 2004. *Indoor air quality: A guide for a facility manager.* Lilburn, GA: The Fairmont Press Inc.

Baumann, Oliver. 2009. 'Integrated Design – Delivery and Operations of Net-Zero Energy Buildings.' Powerpoint presentation to the U.S. Department of Energy, October.

Becker, Franklin and Steele, Fritz. 1995. *Workplace by Design.* San Francisco: Jossey-Bass Inc

Berezan, Ron. 2007. 'The Edible Landscape: An Urban Farming Renaissance?' *The Canadian Organic Grower,* Fall 2007.

Bergethon, Kriss. 2011. 'More Efficient and Affordable Solar Power: Developments Changing the Industry.' Modified May 22.

Bhatt, Vikram et al. 2005. *Making the Edible Landscape: a Study of Urban Agriculture in Montreal.* Canada: Minimum Cost Housing Group, McGill University School of Architecture.

Bosch Thermotechnology. 2011. 'Solar Flat Plate Collectors.' Accessed Jun 21, 2011.

British Columbia Institute of Technology (BCIT). 2009. 'The Centre for Architectural Ecology: Collaborations in Green Roofs and Living Walls.' Accessed in 2009.

Burney, Teresa. 2010. 'Good Things Come in Small Packages,' *Builder Magazine.* February.

California Energy Commission. 2011. 'Passive Solar Design: Proper Orientation'. Accessed June 25.

Canadian Mortgage and Housing Corporation (CMHC). 2010. 'Buying a Water-Efficient Toilet.' Last modified 2010.

Canadian Mortgage and Housing Corporation(CMHC). 2011a. 'Building Housing Incrementally.' Accessed May 18, 2011.

Canadian Mortgage and Housing Corporation(CMHC). 2011b. 'Install Water Conserving Fixtures.' Accessed July 7.

Center for Strategic & International Studies (CSIS). 2010. 'Global Aging Initiative,' Accessed May 9, 2011.

Chan, Yenna. 2007. *Small Environments: Contemporary Design in Detail.* Gloucester: Rockport.

City of Portland, Bureau of Planning and Sustainability. 2011. 'Rainwater Harvesting.' Accessed July 7.

City of Vancouver. 2011. 'Edible Landscaping.' Brochure Online. Accessed July 5.

Composite Panel Association. 2011. 'Composite Wood Products: Green by Nature.' Accessed June 30, 2011.

Consexto Architects. 2010. 'Closet House, Matosinhos, Portugal.' Accessed June 16, 2011

Craig, Barry, Bourassa, Andre, Ruest, Ken, Hill, Duncan, and Marshall, Sandra. 2004. *Indoor air quality in interior environments.* Ottawa, Ontario, Canada: Canadian Mortgage and Housing Corporation

Davies, Colin. 2005. *The Prefabricated Home.* Great Britain: Cromwell Press.

Davis and Wilson. 2010. 'Choosing a Soil Amendment.' Colorado State University. Last modified May 12.

De Garrido, Luis. 2008. Essay within [Duran, Sergi. 2008. *New Prefab Architecture.* Barcelona: Equipo Loft Publications.]

Dietsch, Deborah K. 2008. *Live/Work: Working at Home, Living at Work.* Singapore: Abrams

Dunnett, Nigel and Kingsbury, Noel. 2008. *Planting Green Roofs and Living Walls.* Portland, Cambridge: Timber Press.

Duran, Sergi. 2008. *New Prefab Architecture.* Barcelona: Equipo Loft Publications.

Durisol. 2011. 'Concrete Wood Forms.' Accessed June 30, 2011.

Edil, Tuncer and Schaertl, Greg. 2010. 'Study: Recycled Aggregate Summary Report.' *Mining Media International,* March 9.

Elliott, Monica. 2005. 'Adaptable Architecture,' *Industrial Engineer Magazine,* September.

Encyclopaedia Britannica, *Heat Transfer,* 2011b, Encyclopaedia Britannica Online, Accessed June 9 2011.

Encyclopaedia Britannica, *Homeostasis,* 2011a. Encyclopaedia Britannica Online, Accessed June 9 2011.

Environmental Protection Agency (EPA). 2011. 'WaterSense: Outdoor Water Use in the United States.' Last modified July 7.

Flanigan, Lorraine. 2011. 'All About Xeriscaping.' *Canadian Gardening Magazine Online.* Acessed July 18, 2011.

FlorDepot. 2011a. 'Pitch Roofs Up to 20 Degrees.' *FlorDepot International.* Accessed July 12, 2011.

FlorDepot. 2011b. 'Pitch Roofs Up to 45 Degrees.' *FlorDepot International.* Accessed July 12, 2011.

Friedman, Avi. 2001. *The Grow Home.* Ithaca; McGill-Queen's University Press: Montreal.

Friedman, Avi. 2002. 'The Adaptable House: Designing Homes for Change.' New York: McGraw-Hill.

Friedman, Avi. 2005. *Homes Within Reach: A Guide to the Planning, Design, and Construction of Affordable Homes and Communities.* New Jersey: John Wiley & Sons.

Friedman, Avi. 2007. *Sustainable Residential Development.* New York: McGraw-Hill.

Fuad-Luke, Alastair. 2004. *The Eco-Design Handbook.* London: Thames & Hudson.

Galvagni, Flavio. 2011. 'Portable Prefabs: Location-Independent Modular Homes.' Accessed Jun 16, 2011.

Garcia, Maria. 2009. 'Building Products Made of Recycled Materials in the North American Home Building Industry.' Unpublished Master's Report. McGill University, School of Architecture.

Garnett, Larry. 2011. 'Expandable Designs.' *Professional Builder Magazine,* March.

Gonchar, AIA. 2008. 'Some Assembly Required,' *Architectural Record Magazine,* September. Vol. 196, No. 9.

Gonchar, Joann. 2010. 'Zeroing In on Net-Zero Energy.' *Architectural Record,* December 2010, Vol. 198 Issue 12.

Green Venture. 2011. 'Xeriscaping.' Accessed July 18, 2011.

GreenRoofs. 2011. *Greenroofs 101.*

GRHC. Green Roofs for Healthy Cities. 2009. 'About Green Roofs.' Last updated December 8, 2009.

Gutierrez, Thelma. 2008. 'Tiny Homes Big in Down Economy,' CNN television report. Oct. 22. Accessed May 11, 2011.

Haeg, Fritz. 2010. *Edible Estates: Attack on the Front Lawn.* New York: Bellerophon Publications, Inc.

Harvey, Danny. 2006. *A Handbook on Low-Energy Buildings and District-Energy Systems; Fundamentals, Techniques, and Examples.* London and Sterling, VA: Earthscan. Hasanain et al. 2003.

Headwaters, Inc. 2005. 'Fly Ash for Concrete.' Headwaters Resources Online. Accessed June 30, 2011.

Herwig, Oliver. 2008. *Universal Design: solutions for a barrier-free living.* Birkhauser Verlag AG: Berlin.

HVAC Home. 2006. 'What is HVAC?' Last Modified March 21.

ICOST: 8th International Conference on Smart Homes and Health Telematics. 2010. 'Aging Friendly Technology for Health and Independence.' June 22-24. Seoul, Korea.

Jaffe, Justin. 2011. 'U.S. Home Office 2011 - 2015 Forecast: Recovery Drives Interest in IT as Home Office Households Adjust to New Economic Realities.' International Data Centre Online.

JamesHardie Building Products Inc. 2011. 'Product Performance.' Accessed June 30.

Johnston and Gibson. 2010. *Toward a Zero Energy Home; a complete guide to energy self-sufficiency at home.* United States: The Taunton Press.

Johnston, David and Gibson, Scott. 2008. *Green from the Ground Up: Sustainable, Healthy, and Energy-efficient Home Construction.* Newtown: The Taunton Press.

Juneau, Graham. 2011. 'Solar Air Heating

Systems.'

Ontario Ministry of Agriculture, Food and Rural Affairs. Last modified April 11.

Keeler, Marian and Burke, Bill. 2009. *Fundamentals of Integrated Design for Sustainable Building.* Hoboken, NJ, U.S.A.: John Wily & Sons, Inc.

Khan, Tanya. 2010. 'Kentucky Bluegrass Vs. Fescue.' *GardenGuides.com.* Accessed July 19, 2011.

Klimchuk, Amanda. 2008. 'Xeriscaping: Procedure, Analysis and Recommendation.' *The Living Home Online,* July 08.

Kourik, Robert. 2004. *Designing and Maintaining your Edible Landscape Naturally.* Hampshire, U.K.: Permanent Publications

Kurutz, Steven. 2008. 'The Next Little Thing?' *NY Times,* Sept. 10. Accessed May 11, 2011.

Kwok, Alison and Grondzik, Walter. 2007. *The Green Studio Handbook: Environmental Strategies for Schematic Design.* Amsterdam: Elsevier Architectural Press.

Landreville, Maude. 2005. *Toitures vertes a la montrealaise: rapport de recherché sure l'implantation de toits vertes a Montreal.* Montreal, Quebec: Societe de developpement communautaire de Montreal.

Lawlor, Drue and Thomas, Michael A.. 2008. *Residential Design for Aging In Place.* New Jersey: John Wiley & Sons.

Lee, Marlene and Mather, Mark. 2008. 'Population Bulletin: U.S. Labor Force Trends' *The Population Reference Bureau, Vol. 63, No.2.* June. Accessed May 02, 2011.

Losantos, Agata. 2006. *Mini House Now.* Spain: Loft.

Louisiana-Pacific Cor. 2011. 'Products.' Accessed June 30.

Louv, Richard. 2005. *Last Child in the Woods: Saving Our Children from Nature-Deficit Disorder.* North Carolina: Algonquin Books.

Lovgren, Stefan. 2005. 'Spray-On Solar-Power Cells Are True Breakthrough.' *National Geographic News,* January 14.

Lumeta Incorporated. 2011. 'Powerply ™.' Accessed June 21.

Macht, William P., 2010. 'Modular Net-Zero-Energy Townhouses,' *Urban Land, July/ August 2010.*

MatrixAir, Matrix Energy. 2009. 'Backpass Solar Air Heating Collector System.' Accessed June 21, 2011.

Mauritius EcoBuilding. 2008. A Business Division of Alive2green. 'Roofs.'

Miller, Charlie. 2010. 'Extensive Green Roofs.' *Whole Building Design Guide: National Institute of Building Sciences,* Last updated June 11, 2010.

Millet, Fred. 2010. 'Greenbuild Video: Demonstration of Pleotint's Thermochromic Glass.' *Glass Magazine Online Video,* November 22, 2010.

Morcos, Natalie. 2009. 'Exploring Small Residential Spaces.' Unpublished Master's Report, McGill University, School of Architecture.

Nastase, Ilinca and Meslem, Amina. 2010. 'Lobed Grilles for High Mixing Ventilation – An Experimental Analysis in a Full Scale Model Room.' *Building and Environment Magazine,* March 2011, vol. 46, issue 3, pgs

547 – 555.

Nature First, U.K. 2011a. 'Tree Size Guide.' Accessed July 13, 2011.

Nature First, U.K. 2011b. 'Tree Moving.' Accessed July 13, 2011.

Nio, Ivan and Kuenzli, Peter. 2003. *Parasite Paradise: A Manifesto for Temporary Architecture and Flexible Urbanism.* NAi Publishers: Leidsche.

Oliver, Connie. 2011. 'Create an airy feel with creative techniques.' *Global Winnipeg.* Accessed June 16, 2011.

Oregon State University. 2011. 'Edible Landscaping.' *Oregon State University Master Gardner.* Accessed July 5.

Palmer, Jasmine and Ward, Stephen. 2010. 'The Adaptable House.' Accessed May 16, 2011.

Parker, Ken. 2000. 'Multi-generational Living: Design for Ageing.' IFA Fourth Global Conference on Ageing. Summarized in Journal Ageing International. 1999-2000. vol 25, page 90 – 100.

Peck, Steven and Kuhn, Monica. 2008. 'CMHC Design Guidelines for Green Roofs.' Accessed July 12, 2011.

Penn, Mark. 2008 *Microtrends: Suprising Tales of the Way We Live Today.* U.K.: Penguin.

Plastic Lumber Depot. 2011. 'Plastic Lumber Products.' Accessed June 30.

Population Reference Bureau (PRB). 2008. '2008 World Population Data Sheet.' Accessed May 9, 2011.

Portland Cement Association. 2009. 'Sustainable Development with Concrete.' Accessed June 30, 2011.

Public Works and Government Services Canada 2009. *The environmentally responsible construction and renovation handbook.*

Quantum Solar Power. 2011. 'A Comparison of PV Technologies.' Accessed June 21.

Rastra. 2011. 'ICF – Insulated Concrete Forms / Compound ICF.' Accessed June 30, 2011.

REcampus. 2011. 'Principles of Air Conditioning.' Accessed June 29.

Renewable Energy United Kingdom (REUK). 2008. 'Flush Toilet With Rain Water.' Last modified Feb 21, 2008.

Rosenthal, Elisabeth. 2008. 'No Furnaces but Heat Aplenty in 'Passive Houses''. *The New York Times,* December 26.

Salomon, Emily. 2010. 'Housing Policy Solutions to Support Aging in Place,' AARP Public Policy Institute. Last Modified in March, 2010.

Sassi, Paola. 2006. *Strategies for Sustainable Architecture.* Abingdon: Taylor & Francis.

SCAFCO Steel Stud Mfg. Co. 2009. 'Steel Studs: The Superior Alternative to Wood.' Accessed June 30, 2011.

Schaeffer, J. 2005. *The Real Goods Solar Living Sourcebook: Your Complete Guide to Renewable Energy technologies and Sustainable Living.* 12th ed. Gabriola Island, BC: New Society Publishers.

ScienceDaily. 2009. 'Science Suggests Access To Nature is Essential to Human Health.' *University of Illinois at Urbana-Champaign,* Feb 19, 2009. Accessed July 12, 2011.

Senbel, Maged. 1995. 'Working at Home and Sustainable Living: Architecture and Planning Implications.' Unpublished Master's Thesis, McGill University.

Shirley-Smith, C. And Butler, D. 2007. 'Paper:

Water Management at BedZED: Some Lessons.' *Institute of Civil Engineers.* Accessed July 7, 2011.

Sliva, Veronica. 2011. 'Xeriscaping.' *HGTV Online,* Shaw Media Inc. Accessed July 18, 2011.

SmartGlass International. 2010. 'What is Electrochromic Glass?'. Accessed June 28.

Smith, Peter. 2003. *Sustainability at the Cutting Edge.* Oxford: Architectural Press

Snodgrass, Edmund and McIntyre, Linda. 2010. *The Green Roof Manual.* London: The Timber Press.

Solar Air Heating. 2011. 'Solar Air Heating Options Compared, and Recommendations.' Accessed June 21, 2011.

Solar Panels Plus. 2007. 'Passive Solar Tracking.' Accessed June 21, 2011.

Solomon, Christopher. 2011. 'Hot New-Home Trends for 2011.' *MSN Real Estate Online.* Accessed July 20, 2011.

Stein, Benjamin and Reynolds, John. 2000. *Mechanical and Electrical Equipment for Buildings.* New York: John Wiley & Sons.

Strongman, Cathy. 2008. *The Sustainable Home: The Essential Guide to Eco Building, Renovation and Decoration.* London: Merrell Publishers.

Studio Aisslinger. 2011. ' the LoftCube project.' Accessed Jun 16, 2011.

Sullivan, Jennifer. 2011. 'Go Expandable: Homes that Grow With You.' *Rhode Island Home and Design Magazine.* Accessed on May 18, 2011.

Sustainable Sources. 2011e. 'Flyash Concrete.' Accessed June 30.

Sustainable Sources. 2011a. 'Ductwork.' Accessed June 23.

Sustainable Sources. 2011b. 'Passive Solar Design.' Accessed June 28.

Sustainable Sources. 2011c. 'Ridge and Soffit Venting.' Accessed June 23.

Sustainable Sources. 2011d. 'Solar Hot Water, Heating and Cooling Systems.' Accessed June 23.

Takaharu and Yui Tezuka. 2011a. 'Eaves House.' Accessed June 16, 2011.

Takaharu and Yui Tezuka. 2011b. 'Roof House.' Accessed June 16, 2011.

Tanha, Ali. 2010. 'Net-Zero Apartment Buildings.' Unpublished Master's Report. McGill University, School of Architecture.

Taylors Recycled Plastic Products Inc. 2011. 'About Products.' Accessed June 30.

Trulove, James and Cha, Ray. 2007. *PreFabNow,* Washington: Collins Design.

Vinyl Siding Institute. 2009. 'About Vinyl Siding.' Accessed June 30, 2011.

Williams, Anna. 2008. 'Facts About Thin Film Solar Panels.' Last modified December 02.

World Health Organization, 2010. 'Global Health Indicators,' Accessed on May 11, 2011.

Zhao, Jing. 2001. 'Intergenerational Living and Housing.' Unpublished Master's Report, McGill University, School of Architecture.

Project references

CHAPTER 1
House S, Breda
Contemporarist, 'S House by Grosfeld van der Architecten', Accessed on May 4, 2011.
Grosfeld van der Architecten, 'Woonhuis S', Accessed on May 4, 2011. URL:
Saieh, Nico. 'House S/Grosfeld van der Velde Architecten', Accessed on May 4, 2011.

Intexure Live-Work Studio
DesignMilk, 'Live-Work Studio in Texas by Intexure', Accessed on May 6, 2011.
Meinhold, Bridgette, 'Intexure's Architecture Office Doubles as Beautiful Eco Home', Last updated Jan 14, 2011. Accessed on May 6, 2011.
Singhal, Sumit, 'Intexure LiveWork Studio in Houston', last Updated on Feb 3, 2011. Accessed on May 6, 2011.

CHAPTER 2
Villa Deys
Architectenweb, 'Villa Deys, Rhenen', Accessed on May 17, 2011.
Modern Residential Design, 'Paul de Ruiter - Villa Deys'. Accessed on May 17 2011.
Saieh, Nico, 'Villa Deys / Paul de Ruiter', Last updated Apr 12, 2009. Accessed on May 15, 2011.

CHAPTER 3
Jones House
Architonic, 'Haus Jones'. Accessed on May 20, 2011.
Architectuul, 'Haus Jones' on May 20, 2011.
Heinze, 'Haus Jones: Vier Genrationen-auHs in Goldenen Grund', Accessed on May 20, 2011.

Ravine Residence
'The Ravine Residence by Cindy Rendely Architecture', Last updated on Nov 26, 2009. Accessed on May 2011.
Desnoyer, Michelle, 'Power of Three - Three generations reside in Toronto ravine home', Hardwood Floors (Aug/September 2008).

CHAPTER 4
L41 Home
Busyboo, 'Small Prefab: L41 Home for All', Last modified Nov 2010. Accessed on May 25, 2011.
Cook + Fox, 'L41 Home for All', Last modified 2010. Accessed on May 25, 2011.
Gold, Kerrey, 'Have you got 220 square feet to spare?', Last modified March 2010. Accessed on May 25, 2011.
Meinhold, Bridgette, 'The L41 Prefab Home Packs a Whole Lot into a Tiny Space', Last modified July 2010. Accessed on May 25, 2011.

House to Catch the Forest
Basalt, David, 'House to catch the forest/Tezuka Architects', Last modified Mar 2009.
Best House Design, 'House to catch the forest - Tezuka Architects', Last modified 2010.
Galindo, Michelle, 'House to Catch the Forest', *Contemporary Prefab Houses*. Germany: Braun Publishing, 2011.

CHAPTER 5
Butler House
Specifier, 'Butler House by Andrew Maynard Architects', accessed on May 26, 2011.
Michler, Andrew, 'Andrew Maynard Unveils Beautiful Redesigned Warehouse Home'. Last modified Oct 2010.

Live Work Home
Cook+Fox Architects, 'Live/work/Home', accessed May 24, 2011.
Lee, Evelyn, 'Adaptable Live Work Home Wrapped With a Beautiful Perforated Façade', Inhabitant. Last Modified Accessed May 24, 2011.
Progetti, 'Live Work Home', Last Updated May 19 2009. Accessed on May 24, 2011.

CHAPTER 6
MOMO – Modern Modular
Grasshopper MOMO, 'MOMO', Accessed May 29, 2011.
Baekdal, Thomas, 'Momo Prefab', Accessed May 28, 2011.
Johnnu, 'MOMO Modular by Grasshopper Studio', Accessed May 29, 2011.

Prefab LightHouses
MIMOA, 'Lighthouses' by Berend Schiphorst
Architectuur.nl, 'Lighthouses, verdichten de binnenstad met dakophbouwen', Last Updated: Oct 31, 2006. Accessed on May 27, 2011.
Staat In Groningen, 'Lighthouses', Accessed on May 27, 2011.

CHAPTER 7
Wood House in Caviano
ArchiCentral, 'Wood House//Caviano// Switzerland//Wespi De Meuron'. Last updated Apr 9, 2009. Accessed on May 30, 2011.
Saieh, Nico, 'Wood House in Caviano', Last Updated Feb 14, 2009. Assessed on May 30, 2011.

Zufferey House
Saieh, Nico, 'Zufferey House / Nunatak Sàrl Architectes', accessed May 24, 2011.
BusyBoo, 'Prefab-Zufferey House', accessed May 24, 2011.

CHAPTER 8
Narrow House
Designboom. 'Narrow house by Ohad Yehieli'. Accessed on June 9, 2011.
Arch-times. 'Narrow house by Ohad Yehieli'. Accessed on June 9, 2011.

Layer House
Modern Residential Design. 'Hiroaki Ohtani - Kobe Layer House'. Accessed on June 8, 2011.
Pollock, Naomi. 'The Layer House'. Accessed on June 8, 2011.

CHAPTER 9
LoftCube
Fehrenbacher, Jill, May 2005, 'LOFTCUBE: Prefab for Rooftops'. Accessed Jun 7, 2011.
Loftcube. Accessed June 7, 2011.

FloorNature. 'LoftCube. Werner Assigner'. Accessed on June 8, 2011.

Arado weeHouse
Trendier. 'Small Prefab home- modern weeHouse makes a big Impression'. Accessed on June 7, 2011.
Rich, Sarah. 'PREFAB FRIDAY: WeeHouse', Inhabitant. Last Modified June 16, 2006. Accessed on June 7, 2011.
WeeHouse. 'Preliminary Information'. Accessed on June 8, 2011.

CHAPTER 10
NEXTHouse
Henry, Christopher, 'NEXTHouse/ David Vandervort Architects', Last Updated Jun 2, 2011. Accessed on Jun 23, 2011.
The Architecture 4 Us, 'The Eco Construction of NEXTHouse David Vandervort Architects'. Last updated June 3 2011. Accessed June 22, 2011.
David Vernderort Architects, 'NEXTHouse - Seattle, WA', Last Updated Jan 20, 2009. Accessed on June 23, 2011.

Steel Study House II
Rosenberg, Andrew, 'Steel Study House II', Accessed February 1, 2012.

CHAPTER 11
Lighthouse
Robson, Sheppard, 'The LightHouse', Last Updated 2008. Accessed on June 21, 2011.
Chapa, Jorge, 'The Lighthouse: The UK's first zero-emission home', last updated June 18, 2007. Accessed on June 21, 2011.
archiCentral, 'The lighthouse// Sheppard Robson: UK's First Net Zero Carbon Home', Last Updated on Jan 21, 2008. Accessed on Jun 21, 2011. UltimateHouse, 'Lighthouse, UK', last updated on Oct 24, 2007. Accessed on June 21, 2011.

Sunlighthouse
Henry, Christopher, '700 Palms Residence/ Ehrilich Architects', Last updated March 1, 2011. Accessed on June 22, 2011.
Michler, Andrew, 'Velux Sunglighthouse is Austria's First Net-Zero Energy and Carbon House', Last updated Jun 7, 2011. Accessed on Jun 22, 2011.
OpenBuildings, 'Velux Sunglighthouse', Accessed on June 22, 2011.

CHAPTER 12
Trial Bay House
Specifier, 'Trial Bay House by HBV Architects'. Accessed July 6, 2011.
Minner, Kelly. 'Trial Bay House / James Jones/ HBV Architects' Archdaily. Accessed July 6, 2011.
Architects, HBV. 'Trial Bay House - Architecture Gallery - Australian Institute of Architects, The Voice of Australian Architecture.' Australian Institute of Architects. Accessed July 7, 2011.
'Tassie home wins best design Tasmania News.' The Mercury - News, Views, Sports, Lifestyle and Fun - The Voice of Tasmania. Accessed July 7, 2011.

CHAPTER 13
Home for Life/Activehouse
Purcell, Andrew, 'Zero-carbon eco home is light years ahead'. Last updated on May 2009. Accessed on June 28, 2011.

Architecture Today, 'AART: Active House (or Home for Life), Aarhus, Denmark'. Last updated Jan 1 2009, accessed on June 28, 2011.

ActiveHouse, 'Home for Life'. Accessed on June 28, 2011.

Den, Tirsdag, 'Bolig for livet/Home for life by AART'. Last Updated April 2010. Accessed on June 28, 2011.

Malibu 5
Architecture Page, 'Malibu 5', Accessed on June 29, 2011.

Kanner Architects, 'Malibu 5 House', Accessed on June 29, 2011.

CHAPTER 14
OS House
Bernstein, Fred A. 'On Location - The Lake House Effect - NYTimes.com.' The New York Times - Breaking News, World News & Multimedia. Accessed July 7, 2011.

Kolleeny, Jane. 'OS House - Green Building and Environmental Project Case Studies - GreenSource Magazine.' Green building, LEED projects and sustainable design -- commercial green buildings, building performance and green homes -- sustainable materials and green building products -- GreenSource Magazine. Accessed July 7, 2011.

Michler, Andrew. 'LEED Platinum House With a Brilliant Modernist Design | Inhabitat - Green Design Will Save the World.' Green design will save the world | Inhabitat. Accessed July 7, 2011.

'OS House, Racine, WI by Johnsen Schmaling Architects.' Archinnovations.com Front Page. Accessed July 7, 2011.

'Racine Post: 'Green' home brings modern design to historic district.' Racine Post. Accessed July 7, 2011.

'The American Institute of Architects - Replace.' The American Institute of Architects - Replace. Sccessed July 7, 2011.

Pryor House
'Bates Masi Architects Home.' Bates Masi Architects. Accessed July 8, 2011. 'Prefab Pryor House | Busyboo Design Blog.' Interior Design Style, Prefab Homes Design, Modern Architecture. Accessed July 8, 2011.

Meinhold, Bridgette. 'Bates Masi Prefab Home Wins AIA Award | Inhabitat - Green Design Will Save the World.' Green design will save the world | Inhabitat. Accessed July 8, 2011.

Saeih, Nico. 'Pryor Residence / Bates Masi Architects'. Archdaily. Accessed July 8, 2011.

CHAPTER 15
Big Dig House
Single Speed Design. 'Big Dig House .' Accessed July 13, 2011.

DiCamillo, Kara, Newport, and Rhode Island. "The Big Dig' Gets Recycled : TreeHugger.' TreeHugger. Accessed July 13, 2011.

Dolden, Ginger. 'Big Dig House: Recycled Residence Reaches Completion | Inhabitat - Green Design Will Save the World.' Green design will save the world | Inhabitat. Accessed July 13, 2011.

'House Tour: Inside Marc and Lana's Big Dig House Lexington, Massachusets | Apartment Therapy Boston.' Apartment Therapy. Accessed July 13, 2011.

Shulman, Ken. 'From Highway to Home | Metropolis Magazine.' Metropolis Magazine Celebrating 30. July 13, 2011.

CHAPTER 16
Villa 4.0
Arets, Wiel. 'Dezeen » Blog Archive » Villa 4.0 by Dick van Gameren.' Dezeen architecture and design magazine. Accessed July 21, 2011.

'Dick van Gameren.' Dick van Gameren architecten. Accessed July 21, 2011.

Laylin, Tafline. 'Villa 4.0: Hexagonal Dutch Home Gets a Green Facelift | Inhabitat - Green Design Will Save the World.' Inhabitat - Green Design Will Save the World. Accessed July 21, 2011. URL:

'Villa 4.0: Renovated sustainable house for eco denizens.' Ecofriend : Green Living. Accessed July 21, 2011.

7ten Project
'Project7ten Goes for Platinum, Draws Celebrity Crowd.' Jetson Green | Design-oriented site for sustainable homes, natural materials, and green technology. Accessed July 21, 2011.

'710 Milwood Avenue.' project710. Accessed July 21, 2011.

'Green Home in California - LEED Platinum-Certified Project7ten home | Green.' Trendir - Home Decorating Trends magazine. Accessed July 21, 2011.

Lee, Evelyn. 'PROJECT7TEN HOUSE Gets LEED Platinum | Inhabitat - Green Design Will Save the World.' Inhabitat - Green Design Will Save the World. Accessed July 21, 2011.

'Project7ten To Be The First Ever Famed Los Angeles 'ECO-HOME' To Be Sold On eBay.' Press Release Distribution - Submit Press Releases Online - PRWeb. Accessed July 21, 2011.

CHAPTER 17
House Ocho
'House Ocho with a Lively Green Roof .' Jetson Green | Design-oriented site for sustainable homes, natural materials, and green technology. Accessed July 15, 2011.

AECCafe. 'AECCafe.' Accessed July 15, 2011.

'Sustainable House Ocho by Feldman Architecture | HomeDSGN, a daily source for inspiration and fresh ideas on interior design and home decoration.' Interior Design, Architecture and Contemporary Homes Magazine – HomeDSGN. Accessed July 15, 2011.

'Extensive Residential Green Roof by Rana Creek Filters and Stores Water | Green.' Trendir - Home Decorating Trends magazine. Accessed July 15, 2011.

'Greening Rooftops for Sustainable Communities.' Green Roofs for Healthy Cities. Accessed July 15, 2011.

'Sustainable House Ocho by Feldman Architecture | architecture 4 us.' Architecture 4 Us. Accessed July 15, 2011.

Zimmer, Lori. 'Green Roof House Ocho is a

Santa Lucia Mountain Retreat | Inhabitat - Green Design Will Save the World.' Inhabitat - Green Design Will Save the World. Accessed July 15, 2011.

Villa Bio
'It Takes a Villa - Homes - Dwell.' Dwell - At Home in the Modern World. Accessed July 14, 2011.

Meinhold, Bridgette. 'Villa Bio: Home With a Cantilevered Living Roof is a Feat of Engineering | Inhabitat - Green Design Will Save the World.' Inhabitat - Green Design Will Save the World. Accessed July 14, 2011.

Saieh, Nico. 'Villa Bio / Enric Ruiz Geli.' Archdaily. Accessed July 13, 2011.

'The Villa Bio | Barcelona Spain | Buzz Beast | Digital Lifestyle Magazine.' Buzz Beast. Accessed July 14, 2011.

'Villa Bio – Contemporary House with Hydroponic Rooftop Garden | DigsDigs.' Interior Decorating, Home Design, Room Ideas - DigsDigs. Accessed July 14, 2011.

CHAPTER 18
OS House
'Green Dream Home | Casa OS by Nolaster Architects « G Living | Dark Twisted Space Monkies Go Green.' G Living | Dark Twisted Space Monkies Go Green. Accessed July 18, 2011.

Saieh, Nico. 'OS House / NOLASTER / ArchDaily.' Archdaily. Accessed July 18, 2011.

Trotter, Cate. 'CASA OS Spanish Green House by Nolaster Architects | Inhabitat - Green Design Will Save the World.' Inhabitat - Green Design Will Save the World. Accessed July 18, 2011.

'Milimetdesign- ArchitectureMagazine' Accessed July 18, 2011.

Rantilla Residence
'Sloped Terrain House - Modern Industrial Meets Nature | Modern House Designs.' Trendir - Home Decorating Trends magazine. Accessed July 19, 2011.

Stefan, and posted in Architecture. 'The Rantilla residence.' Home decorating trends- Interior design & home design. Accessed July 19, 2011.

'The Rantilla Residence by Michael Rantilla.' CONTEMPORIST. Accessed July 19, 2011.

CHAPTER 19
Ross Street House
'Aligned with the Sun in Wisconsin | Architects and Artisans.' Architects and Artisans | Thoughtful Design for a Sustainable World. Accessed July 26, 2011.

'Carol & Fred's Modern Eco Home Green Tour | Apartment Therapy Re-Nest.' Apartment Therapy Re-Nest. Accessed July 26, 2011.

'The Ross Street House by Richard Wittschiebe Hand Architects » CONTEMPORIST.' CONTEMPORIST. Accessed July 26, 2011.

Vaughn, Katie. 'Thoroughly Modern - Madison Magazine - March 2011.' Madison, WI - Shopping, Arts, Dining, Events, Business, Best Of. Accessed July 26, 2011.

Wong, Kenneth. 'When it Comes to LEED, Platinum is the New Green | Cadalyst.' Cadalyst | Cadalyst. Accessed July 26, 2011.

Adams Fleming House
'Beautiful Adams Fleming House in Toronto by

Levitt Goodman Architects.' Accessed July 26, 2011.

Andreea, Mocanu. 'Auto-Body Shop Transformation-The Adams Fleming House.' Home decorating trends- Interior design & home design. Accessed July 26, 2011.

Henry, Christopher. 'Adams Fleming House / Levitt Goodman Architects.' ArchDaily. Accessed July 26, 2011.

'The Adams Fleming House' HomeDesignDecorates. Accessed July 26, 2011.

'The Adams Fleming House by Levitt Goodman Architects.' Architecturas.com. Accessed July 26, 2011.

CHAPTER 20
Residence for a Briard

'House and Design: Briard Green Hybrid Residence by Sander Architects.' House and Design. Accessed July 21, 2011.

'Sander Architects - Residence Briard, a 'Hybrid House'.' Archinnovations.com. Accessed July 21, 2011.

Deepa. 'Residence for a Briard - The Greenest Hybrid House ever built in California.' Greenlaunches.com. Accessed July 21, 2011.

Sander Architects. 'Residential Projects- Residence for a Briard.' Accessed July 21, 2011.

Jacobson Residence

'Build it Green Home is Equal Parts Stylish and Smart I Local Remodeling.' Home Remodeling Contractors - View Remodel Ideas, Get Estimates - CalFinder. Accessed July 21, 2011.

'Green Inside and Out in the Valley.' World Green® - The Sustainability Social Network. Accessed July 21, 2011.

'Wick Architecture RESIDENTIAL JACOBSON RESIDENCE.' Wick Architecture and Design. Accessed July 21, 2011.

Project credits

1.1 HOUSE S, BREDA
Designer
Grosfeld van der Velde Architects: Reduitlaan 39, 4814 DC Breda, the Netherlands
www.grosfeldvandervelde.nl

Team
Project architect: Pascal Grosfeld
Team members: Martijn van Bentum, Gideon Beemster, Dimphy Rops-Klaassen
Interior designer: Vormvast Interior Concepts, Breda
Garden designer: Van Kamsteeg Tuinen, Breda
General contractor: J.F. Koks BV. Aannemersbedrijf, Baarle-Nassau
Structural engineering: R2 Constructie Adviesbureau BV., Breda

1.2 INTEXURE LIVE-WORK STUDIO
Designer
Intexure Architects
1815 Southmore Boulevard
Houston Tx, USA.

Team
Principal Designer: Russell Hruska, AIA and Rame Hruska, AIA
Structural Engineer: Hendricks Engineering

2.1 VILLA DEYS
Designer
Architectural office Paul de Ruiter bv
Valschermkade 36 D
1059 CD Amsterdam
The Netherlands

Team
Principal Designer: Paul de Ruiter
Team Members: Michael Noordam, Sander van Veen, Dieter Blok, Lei Coppus, Hannes Ochmann, Mathilde Joosse, Willeke Smit, Monique Verhoef, Bjørn Peters
Advice installations: Halmos bv, Milieukundig onderzoek- en ontwerpbureau BOOM
Lighting advice: Van Dijk en Partners
Interior architect: Architectural office Paul de Ruiter bv
Landscape ecology: Buro Zijaanzicht
Landscape design: Sytze Hager

3.1 JONES HOUSE
Designer
Reinhardt Jung
386 Wilson Street
Darlington NSW 2008
Australia
Tel: +61 2 80343657
Email: mail@reinhardtjung.de

Team
Principal Designers: Alexander Jung & Dagmar Reinhardt
Engineers: Bollinger & Grohmann, Frankfurt
Clients: Katja + Brian Jones

Awards
The Golden House, 2009
Max40 – BDA Prize, 2011

3.2 RAVINE RESIDENCE
Designer
Cindy Rendely Architexture
44 Charles Street West No. 2504
Toronto, Canada M4Y 1R7
Tel: +1 416 924 9696
www.crarchitexture.com

Team
Project Team Members: Cindy Rendely, Jennifer Scholes, Sassan Sanjari
Architecture, Interior and Landscape Design: Cindy Rendely Architexture
Structural Engineers: Zaretsky Consulting Engineers
Mechanical Engineers: Design Air Climate Air
Electrical Engineers: DeRock Electric
General Contractor: S. Eisner, Eisner Murray Ltd.
Site Supervisor: M. Jackson, Eisner Murray Ltd.

4.1 L41 HOME
Designer
Michael Katz, Architect; Janet Crone, Designer
105 W18th Ave Vancouver B.C. Canada V5Y2A6
Tel: +1 604 338 7400
Email: info@katzarchitecture.com
www.katzarchitecture.com

Team
Principal Designers: Michael Katz and Janet Corne

Awards
The Golden House, 2009
Max40 – BDA Prize, 2011

4.2 HOUSE TO CATCH THE FOREST
Designer
Tezuka Architects
1-19-9-3F, Todoroki, Setagayaku
Tokyo, 158-0082
Japan
Tel: +81 3 3703 7056
Email: tez@sepia.ocn.ne.jp

Team
Principal Designer: Takaharu + Yui Tezuka / Tezuka Architects, Masahiro Ikeda / Masahiro Ikeda co., ltd.
Team Members: Takaharu + Yui Tezuka, Masahiro Ikeda, Ryuya Maio
Lighting Designer: Masahide Kakudate/Lighting Architect & associates

5.1 BUTLER HOUSE
Designer
Andrew Maynard Architects
Suit 12 / 397 Smith St.
Melbourne, Victoria
Australia 3000
Tel: +61 3 9969 6323
Email: info@maynardarchitects.com
maynardarchitects.com

Team
Andrew Maynard
Mark Austin
Tommy Joo

5.2 LIVE WORK HOME
Designer
Cook+Fox Architects
641 Avenue of the Americas
New York, NY 10011
USA
Tel: +1 212 477 0287
Email: abobman@cookplusfox.com

Team
Principal Designer: Rick Cook
Team Members: Pam Campbell, Dan Brammer, Caroline Hahn, Eugene Sun, Tyler Caine, Brandon Hendricks, Guido Elgueta, Simon Rearte
Mechanical Engineer: Jaros, Baum & Bolles
Structural Engineer: Severud Associates
Landscape Design: Terrain
Sustainability Consultant: Kevin Stack

Awards
LEED Platinum, Winner- 'From the Ground Up: Innovative Green Homes' Competition (Syracuse University School of Architecture, in partnership with the Syracuse Center of Excellence and Home HeadQuarters Inc.)

6.1 MOMO – MODERN MODULAR
Designer
Grasshopper AB
Firm Address
Sundskajen 6A

216 43 Limhamn
Sweden
Tel: +46 706 969605
Email: thomas.lind@grasshopper.se

Team
Principal Designer: Thomas Lind, Senior
Architect

6.2 PREFAB LIGHTHOUSES
Designer
DAAD Architecten, Beilen
Postbus 5, 9410 AA Beilen
the Netherlands
Tel: +31 593 582450
Email: info@daad.nl

Team
Principal Designer: Rob Hendriks, Eric de Leeuw
Team Members: Geir Eide, Geert de Wrede
Developer: SHP Bouwbedrijven, Groningen
Timber: Alescon Producten en Diensten,
Hoogeveen
Manufacturer: Ingenieursbureau Wassenaar,
Haren
Engineer: Adviesburo JP van der Weele,
Groningen

7.1 WOOD HOUSE IN CAVIANO
Designer
Markus Wespi Jérôme de Meuron architects
BSA
Via G. Branca Masa 9
6578 Caviano
Switzerland
Tel: +41 91 794 17 73
Email: info@wespidemeuron.ch

Team
Principal Designer: Markus Wespi Jérôme de
Meuron architects BSA
Team Members: Markus Wespi & Jérôme de
Meuron
Engineer: Anastasi SA, 6600 Locarno
Structural engineer: IFEC Consulenze SA,
6802 Rivera
Construction: Gebr. Bissig Holzbau,
6460 Altdorf
Master Builder: Ezio Battistini, 6578 Caviano

7.2 ZUFFEREY HOUSE
Designer
NUNATAK Sàrl
CHERVAZ & VASSAUX - Architectes - EPF -
REG.A - FAS - SIA
Rte de Branson 45 - CH-1926 Fully
Valais, Switzerland
Tel. +41 (27) 746 13 37
Email: nunatak@nunatak.ch
www.nunatak.ch

Team
Principal Designers: Roland Vassaux and Joël
Chervaz
Director: Raymond Vassaux
Drafting: Philippe Scrufari, David Cretton,
Philippe Chassot

8.1 NARROW HOUSE
Designer
Ohad Yehieli Architects (OYA)
23rd Kibutz Galuyot, Studio 9
Tel Aviv Jaffa, Israel

Tel: +972 77 552 60 70
Email: OFFICE@OYA.CO.IL

Team
Principal Designers: Ohad Yehieli Architects
Structural Engineering: Itzhak Rokach – Rokach-
Ashkenazi Engineer, Consultant Ltd.

Awards
Influential Architect of the Year 2009 - Finalist
Israeli Design Award 2011 – Residential Project
of the Year – Finalist

8.2 LAYER HOUSE
Designer
Hiroaki Otani
Shimoyamate-dori 4 11 4
Chuo-ku
Kobe 650-0011
Japan

Team
Principal Designer: Hiroaki Ohtani
Structural Design: Hirokazu Toki

9.1 LOFTCUBE
Designer
Loftcube Inc.
409 Petrel Trail
Bradenton, Florida, 34212
USA

Team Members:
Principal Designer: Werner Aisslinger, Architect
Team Members: Christian Friedrich, CEO
Germany
Patricia Staebler, Director of US Operations

9.2 ARADO WEEHOUSE
Designer
Alchemy
856 Raymond Ave. Suite G
St. Paul, MN 55114, USA
Tel: +1 651 647 6650
www.alchemyarchitects.com

Team
Principal Designer: Geoffrey Warner
Intern Architect: Lucas Alm
Furniture Designer: Scott McGlasson
Consultant: Berhard Stroh, Stroh Engineering
Consultant: Josh Chandler, Chandler Exhibits
Consultant: Roger Berggren, Berggren
Fabricating

Awards
AIA Honor Award, MN 2007
Walker Art Center, 'Some Assembly Required:
Contemporary Prefabricated Houses Walker Art
Center', December 2006-September 2007
La Triennale di Milano, 2008

10.1 NEXTHOUSE
Designer
David Vandervort Architects
2000 Fairview Ave E
Suite 103
Seattle, WA 98102, USA
Tel: +1 206 784 1614
www.vandervort.com

Team
Principal Designer: David Vandervort AIA

Builder: Paulsen Construction
www.paulsenconstructioninc.com

10.2 STEEL STUDY HOUSE II
Designer
Archipelontwerpers
Dr. Lelykade 64
2583 CM
The Hague, the Netherlands
Tel: +31 70 338 75 70
Email: vreedenburgh@archipelontwerpers.nl

Team
Principal Designer: Eric Vreedenburgh
Team Members: Coen Bouwmeester,
Guido Zeck
Construction: Eckhart BJKA Engineering
Structural engineering advice: Technisch
Adviesburo Jinstal bv
Contractor: BSB Staalbouw

Award
BTTV Trofee 2011

11.1 LIGHTHOUSE
Designer
Sheppard Robson
77 Parkway
Camden Town
London NW1 7PU, UK
Tel: +44 20 7504 1700
Email: london@sheppardrobson.com

Team
Principal Designer: Sheppard Robson

11.2 SUNLIGHTHOUSE
Designer
Hein-Troy Architects
Burggasse 24/4
A-1070 Wien
Austria
Tel: +43 1 990 84 64
Email: office@juritroy.at

Team
Principal Designer: Juri Troy
Construction Engineers: Merz, Kley and
Partners

Awards
International Chicago Athenaeum Award 2011
Vorarlberg Timber Construction Award 2011
Active Architecture Award 2010

12.1 TRIAL BAY HOUSE
Designer
James Jones, Architect / HBV Architects
22 Salamanca Square
Hobart, Tasmania 7004
Tel: +61 3 6224 9997
Email: hbv@hbvarchitects.com.au

Team
Principal Designer: James Jones (now with
Architectus – www.architectus.com.au)
Team Members: Petrina Moore, Scott
Christensen, Helen Daly
Consultant: Gandy & Roberts Structural
Engineers
Consultant: TBS Electrical & Mechanical
Engineers
Builder: Bennett Construction Pty Ltd

Awards
National Award - Jury Citation - Australian
Institute Of Architects 2010
Named Award: The Robin Boyd Award For
Residential Architecture – Houses
State Award - Jury Citation - Australian Institute
Of Architects 2010
Named Award – The Esmond Dorney Award
For Residential Architecture – Houses

13.1 HOME FOR LIFE/ACTIVEHOUSE
Designer
AART Architects A/S
Aaboulevarden 22, 5th floor
8000 Aarhus, Denmark
Tel: +45 87 30 32 86
Email: aart@aart.dk

Team
Architect: AART Architects A/S
Engineer: Esbensen Consulting Engineers A/S
Developer: Velfac A/S and Velux A/S

13.2 MALIBU 5
Designer
Kanner Architects
1558 10th Street, Suite A
Santa Monica, CA 90401, USA
Tel: +1 310 451 5400 ext 101
www.kannerarch.com

Team
Principal Designer: Stephen H. Kanner, FAIA
Team Members: Damian LeMons, John
Mebasser, Alex Dunn, Jay Fukuzawa
Contractor: Jeff Allyn
Structural Engineer: Tritek Engineering
Civil Engineer: J.K. Associates
Soils Engineer: RJR Engineering Group, Inc.

14.1 OS HOUSE
Designer
Johnsen Schmaling Architects
1699 N. Astor Street
Milwaukee, WI 53202, USA
Tel: +1 414 287 9000
Email: info@johnsenschmaling.com

Team
Principal Designer: Brian Johnsen and Sebastian
Schmaling
Team Member: Nick Woods
Structural Engineer: Larson Engineering
Landscape Architect: Dan Reisdorf

Awards
Annual Design Review Award, ARCHITECT, 2011
AIA/COTE Top Ten Green Award, 2011
National AIA Housing Design Award, 2011
AIA Wisconsin Honor Award, 2011
Residential Architect Design Award, 2011
Custom Home Design Merit Award, 2011
Architype Review Award, 2011

14.2 PRYOR HOUSE
Designer
Bates Masi Architects
138 Main St, PO Box 510
Sag Harbor, NY 11963
Tel: +1 631 725 0229
Email: info@batesmasi.com

Team
Principal Designer: Paul Masi

Landscape Design: Coen & Partners
Structural Engineer: Steven L. Maresca

Awards
2009 AIA Long Island ArchiAward, 2010 AIA
NYS Award of Merit
2010 AIA Peconic Honor Award, 2010
International Design Awards Hon. Mention

15.1 BIG DIG HOUSE
Designer
SsD (Single Speed Design)
171 Brookline Street
Cambridge, MA 02139, USA
Tel: +1 212 248 7500
Email: info@ssdarchitecture.com

Team
Principal Designers: John Hong & Jinhee Park
Team Members: Erik Carlson, Sadmir Ovcina,
Chris Minor
Structural Design & Construction: Paul Pedini
Structural Engineer: Weidlinger Associates, Inc:

Awards
2006 AIA/BSA Honor Award Citation
2006 AIA/BSA Housing Design Award

16.1 VILLA 4.0
Designer
Dick van Gameren Architecten
Willem Fenengastratt 4b
1096 BN Amsterdam, the Netherlands

Team
Principal Designer: Dick van Gameren
Team Members: Maarten de Geus, Sebastiaan
Kaal, Maarten Peters, Mark Sloof, Justin Fowler,
Helga van Wijk
Interior: IDing (www.iding.nl)
Landscape: Michael van Gessel (www.
michaelvangessel.com)
Construction: BreedID (www.breedid.nl)
Builder: Bouwbedrijf L. Post en Zonen (www.
bouwbedrijfpost.nl)
Building Counseling: Tijs Post (www.tijspost.nl)

16.2 710 PROJECT
Designer
GRAYmatter Architecture
639 East Channel Road
Santa Monica, CA 90402, USA
Tel: +1 310 454 7960
Email: mgray@graymatterarchitecture.com

Team
Principal Designer: Melinda Gray AIA
Team Members: Noreena Manio - Design
partner, Chris Jones – model maker and 3d
modeler, Moritz Freund – Job captain

17.1 HOUSE OCHO
Designer
Feldman Architecture
1126 Folsom St #4
San Francisco, CA 94103, USA
Tel: +1 415 252 1441
Email: info@feldmanarch.com

Team
Principal Designer: Jonathan Feldman
Contractor: Groza Construction
Landscape Design: Loretta Gargan Landscape +
Design And Blasen Landscape Architecture

Lighting Design: Steinbeck Technical Consulting
Engineer: Fulcrum Engineering
Green Roof Consultant: Rana Creek

17.2 VILLA BIO
Designer
Cloud 9 / Enric Ruiz-Geli
Passatge Mercader 10, local 3
08008 Barcelona, Spain
Tel: +34 93 215 0553
Email: enric@e-cloud9.com

Team
Principal Designer: Enric Ruiz-Geli
Team Members: Manel Soler, Laia Jutgla
Structure: Manel Raventós
Interior Design: Manel Soler Caralps
Technical Architect: Arantza Garetaonandia
Structure Constructor: Antonio Diosdado
Installations: Joaquim Ribes Quintana
Natural Roof: Jardines Burés
Landscape Design: Joan Madorell
Glass Work: Cricursa
Glass Rocks: Emiliana Design Estudio
Steel Work: Aluminis Empordł
Visuals: Laia Jutglà
Pavement: Pavindus
Moving Surfaces: Panelite
Fixed Surfaces: Japlac

Awards
Awarded by the Chicago Athenaeum at the
Internation architecture award program, 2007

18.1 OS HOUSE
Designers
Frpo Rodriguez & Oriol Architecture
Rodriguez & Oriol Arquitectos
Cea Bermudez 65 8d
28003 Madrid, Spain
Tel: +34 912838818
Email: frpo@frpo.es

Team
Principal Designers: Pablo Oriol and Fernando
Rodríguez

18.2 RANTILLA RESIDENCE
Designer
Michael Rantilla, AIA
Email: rantmannc@aol.com

Team
Principal Designer: Michael Rantilla
Structural Engineer: Jeff Morrison

Awards
2009 AIA Triangle Honor Award
2009 AIA NC Honor Award
2009 AIA SAR Honor Award (S. Atlantic Region)

19.1 ROSS STREET HOUSE
Designer
Richard Wittschiebe Hand
15 Simpson Street
Atlanta, GA 30308, USA
Tel: +1 678-904-4702
Email: carol@rwhdesign.com

Team
Principal Designer: Carol Richard, AIA, LEED
Homes
Mechanical Engineer: Fred Berg, PE
Landscape Architecture: Lisa Geer, ASLA

Structural: Diana Quinn, PE
General Contractor: Yahara Builders

Awards
Future Landmark Award, 2010, Madison Trust
for Historic Preservation

19.2 ADAMS FLEMING HOUSE
Designer
Levitt Goodman Architects
533 College Street, Suite 301
Toronto, ON M6G 1A8, Canada
Tel: +1 416 203 7600 ext 331

Team
Principal Designer: Janna Levitt
Team Members: Janna Levitt – Partner-in-
Charge, Samantha Scroggie – Project Architect,
Amanda Reed – Intern Architect

Awards
HISE Award for Adams Fleming House, which is
honoured amongst 52 of the 'best, innovative
and intelligently designed houses built within
the last two years' from 36 countries around
the world, 2010.
Design Exchange Award – Residential
Architecture Bronze

20.1 RESIDENCE FOR A BRIARD
Designers
Sander Architects
2434 Lincoln Blvd
Venice, CA 90291, USA

Team
Principal Designer: Whitney Sander
Director of Interiors: Catherine Holliss
Draftsperson: Eli David

20.2 JACOBSON RESIDENCE
Designers
Wick Architecture and Design
1820 Ashmore Place
Los Angeles, CA. 90026, USA
Tel: +1 323.644.9867
Email: davidwick@wickarch.com

Team
Principal Designer: David Wick
Landscape: David Fletcher of Terrain
Water Reclamation: Jenna Didier of
Fountainhead
Structural Engineer: Maged Saad of Maged
Saad & Associates
MEP: T. Nasrollahi, Mechanical Building Systems
Energy Star Inspector: Troy Lindquist of
Alternate Energy Systems
Build It Green Certifier: John Hansen

Picture credits

Index